THE *Complete* GARDEN BIRD

THE Complete GARDEN BIRD

Les Stocker

LEOPARD

This edition published in 1995 by Leopard Books,
an imprint of Random House (UK) Ltd,
20 Vauxhall Bridge Road, London SW1V 2SA

First published in 1991 by Chatto & Windus

ISBN 0 7529 0150 8

Printed in Great Britain by BPC Consumer Books Ltd

Contents

'Bird-Aid' charts

Acknowledgements

Over the years I have been privileged to work with many wild creatures and to meet the caring people who take that special moment out to pick them up. These people together with caring companies have donated money and effort for the welfare of wild birds and other animals, making my dream of a perpetual teaching hospital for wildlife a reality. We have a team of volunteers who clean, feed and give plenty of t.l.c. to our patients. I feel that together we have all made looking after wildlife casualties seem as natural as caring for a sick dog or cat.

This book is the fruit of thirteen years of meeting, healing, caring for and rehabilitating the thousands of wild birds that have arrived on my doorstep. As always, I am grateful to my family for their contribution; Sue, Colin and Andrea have read my manuscripts and commented if they felt I was getting carried away. Di Conger, my very dear friend in Washington DC, cares for many hundreds of orphaned birds every year, and her knowledge, experience and patience have been a mainstay, helping our success with all those previously unrecorded problems which threaten the lives of bird casualties and which I hope I have been able to detail on the following pages. My Mum and Dad I thank for their support, and Catherine Miller for once again typing my manuscript.

I hope this book will make the world a safer place for garden birds, and I would like to thank all those who have helped to make it possible.

PICTURE CREDITS
The author and publishers are grateful for permission to reproduce the following illustrations:
Black and white: Frontispiece, p. 39 Swift Picture Library/Martin King; p. 13, 112 (rt), 115 (left) Frank V. Blackburn; p. 20, 103, 175 Swift Picture Library/Dennis Bright; p. 36 RSPB/E. A. Janes; p. 70 RSPB/C. H. Gomersall; p. 112 (left), 115 (rt) Swift Picture Library/Mike Read.
Drawings: Chapter heads, and p. 5, 35, 60, 79, 110, 131, 141, 165 Guy Troughton.

1 Feathered Encounters

It was five-thirty on Saturday morning, 3 February 1990, when the massive explosion rocked the east side of Aylesbury – the home town of St Tiggywinkles, and base of the Wildlife Hospital Trust. I was on my way to London, volunteered by my wife, Sue, for one of those crack-of-dawn radio programmes, completely oblivious to the holocaust I was leaving behind.

The cement works to the east of Aylesbury manufactures cement from the local limestone in gigantic kilns fired by coal crushed into dust. The building housing the main coal hoppers is usually quite warm and sheltered: a superb roost for the thousands of neighbourhood starlings, pigeons and solitary kestrel. The sleeping birds were unaware of their peril until the blinding, searing fire-ball hit them, just a fraction of a second after one hopper, full of tonnes of coal dust, exploded. The first they knew was the scorching heat melting their feathers and scalding their feet and beaks. They did not even have time to open their eyes, the lids being instantly cau-terised shut by the inferno. Within seconds, thousands of screaming birds were tumbling, helpless, into the eye of the explosion. Many died instantly, some falling into the white-hot ashes of the kilns. Only a few survivors managed to grope their way into dark sooty corners.

There was just one person at the cement works that early in the morning and, luckily, being outside the building he escaped injury, apart from being very obviously shocked by the cataclysm. Showing great courage, he did manage to retrieve about thirty crippled star-lings and a few pigeons before he was forced to leave the dark, impenetrable hole that had once been a building.

At St Tiggywinkles, the phone did not ring. Nobody told us of the hundreds of desperate birds still trapped in that asphyxiating hell.

I returned from my early morning radio stint through a wet and windy countryside, still oblivious to the catastrophe that had occurred almost on our own doorstep. It was still before nine o'clock and as Andy Walton, who runs the everyday animal feeding and cleaning, was due in, I took the opportunity of grabbing a couple of hours' sleep.

I had hardly nodded off when the emergency phone rang and the cement works' man, who had rescued those few birds early on, frantically told Sue about the thousands of birds caught in the blast. He was convinced that there were still hundreds lying injured amongst the carpet of blackened corpses.

I woke to news of the emergency and to the first heavy snowfall of the winter.

Urgently, I mobilised Andy and Nigel Brock, my next-door neighbour, into a rescue team. We were not told how many types of bird were involved but, knowing the large waterfowl populations of the cement works' conservation areas, we could only assume that it was waterfowl that might be involved.

Everything seems to take twice as long when you are in a hurry. After what seemed ages we turned into the works site, a gigantic conglomeration of buildings, steaming furnaces and pipework straight out of science fiction. It seemed deserted, but after a time we were approached and directed through a maze of buildings, silos and railway tracks to underneath a mammoth, revolving pipe 6 metres wide and 400 metres long. Four and a half metres above our heads the joints of the pipe hissed steam and, for yards all around, the snow melted into a slushy quagmire. We could feel the intense heat burning our faces as we stared into the flood, trying to locate the scene of the explosion. Thankfully, the Buckinghamshire fire brigade were on the scene and seemed to have, if not control, at least an understanding of the situation.

A white helmet explained how there was the danger of another explosion and nobody, not even his fire fighters, were allowed near the building until an enormous tonnage of coal and dust had been rendered safe by burning it through the kilns. There was nothing at that time that we could do for any birds still alive in the building. But one other starling had been rescued and was being kept warm in the cab of one of the fire engines.

As I picked the bird up, my heart sank; it looked just like a baby bird, with all its feathers gone and just a sparse amount of down covering its back and sides. Its feet were twisted into grotesque shapes and its eyes were nonexistent. It struck me with horror that if all the casualties were in the same state, then there was nothing I could do to save them. A bird without eyes is completely hopeless. Unlike a mammal, birds have little or no sense of smell and whereas a blind hedgehog, for instance, can cope quite adequately, a blind bird would have to be killed. But I wasn't about to give up and telephoned Sue to get a vet, just on standby, in case we had to take that drastic path.

A fire fighter in his bright yellow jacket materialised out of the snow clutching another tiny, battered starling in his enormous hands. It was in the same condition as the first – a dreadful omen of what we might find when eventually we got into the building.

The other thirty rescued at first light were safely ensconced in a warm shed and were, thankfully, in a much better condition than the first two, although they all had severe feather damage.

The white-helmeted fire chief informed us that it would be at least four or five hours before we could even hope to enter the wrecked building. In view of this, we decided to ferry the casualties we already had back to Aylesbury for treatment.

By the time we reached base and cleared intensive care to handle the casualties, the first two, starlings – the most severely injured – had died. But the others were still jostling one another for position, the natural starling behaviour so often seen at bird tables and feeding centres. True, all their feathers were melted stumps, but as we cleaned and opened their eyelids with warm water, the bright starling stares that greeted us showed that at least most of their eyes had escaped permanent damage. Being asleep at the moment of the blast, with their eyes closed, must have provided perfect protection. A little soothing chloramphenicol ointment in each eye soon eased the eyelids, allowing each bird to see, probably for the first time that fateful day.

Using some new, blunt-ended Spreull's needles, we tube-fed each bird with two and a half millilitres of Beechams Lectade, straight into their proventriculi – a bird's equivalent of

Andy enjoys some hot food while waiting for the all-clear to enter the building

a stomach. Lectade is a rehydrating fluid usually used post-operatively to replace electrolytes lost through shock. In addition, each bird was injected with antibiotics and dexamethasone to try to counter the inevitable damage suffered by their lungs and respiratory systems. In a major crisis like this, with so many birds to rescue, it would not have been practical to rely on just one operative, so all those of us experienced with the procedures set about administering first aid without delay.

It was while concentrating on individual birds that we first noticed another horrifying problem. Some of the starlings appeared to have lost either their top or bottom beak, or often both parts. In fact, the bony parts of the

After the explosion, many of the starlings' beaks started to fall off

beak, the maxillary and mandibular rostra, which are normally covered by horny sheaths, the maxillary and mandibular rhamphothecas, were left exposed when the horny sheaths were missing. I can only assume that these rhampothecas are rather like our own fingernails, with a growing, live portion right at the base. The heat of the blast must have damaged these 'quicks', causing the horny sheath to fall off and leaving the birds with no method of feeding themselves.

Amazingly, the sheaths had simply slid rather than broken off, exposing the short stub of bone. I had recently been working on cementing fractures and other wounds with a specially prepared tissue super-glue. Apply-ing just a dab to the bony stub enabled me to slide the sheath back into place. Then I made the unnerving discovery that all starling beaks are the same size. The horny sheaths of the dead birds therefore made ideal replace-ments for those missing from the survivors. Even the most knowledgeable ornithologists could not tell me if the beaks would regener-ate, but for the moment the 'bionic' birds must have appreciated being able immedi-ately to tuck into bowls of fresh food and water.

A catastrophe like the explosion I've de-scribed, graphically and instantly illustrates the slow, insidious erosion of population that is happening to all our familiar birds. Once they leave the safety of our gardens, they face any number of hazards that are present in industrial and agricultural expanses.

The starling, unloved and often maligned for its garrulous, bustling and sometimes bullying nature, is the most adaptable of birds, pioneering contact with man by its ex-ploitation of the environment man has created. But surely there are so many star-lings that we will not miss a few? Remember the passenger pigeon whose flocks of billions used to block out the American sky? Nobody noticed a few missing until they had all gone the way of the dodo and the great auk – all exterminated by man.

Margaret Mortham, who runs the St Tig-gywinkles office, lives just a few miles from the cement works. On that fateful Saturday

morning she was not woken by the explosion but by the eerie, ominous silence; no starlings raided her bird table as they had done for years. The whole district echoed to the silence as, for once, the small garden birds got first pickings on the table.

Some uninformed people will raise their eyebrows at my deep concern for a few thousand starlings. For once I am just as concerned with numbers as I am deeply concerned with the welfare of each individual casualty. The starling, as I have said, is Britain's hardiest and most adaptable bird and, when you consider that it is also our most effective pest controller, clearing leatherjackets and other pests by the thousand with their non-stop eating frenzy, you begin to realise how important they are. If we were to rely on birds like the starlings and rooks and not on the alchemists' remedies, then the farmers would save a fortune on chemicals and our fields and waterways would be safe for all wild birds and other animals as well as, dare I say it, our children.

The starling is our unsung hero, but also unheralded is the fact that starlings are declining rapidly. We don't yet notice the loss of numbers, but we will. Unless, that is, we garden owners pull out all the stops and make our little pieces of England safe havens from the pesticides and industrial waste of the 'great outdoors' and welcome chemical-free

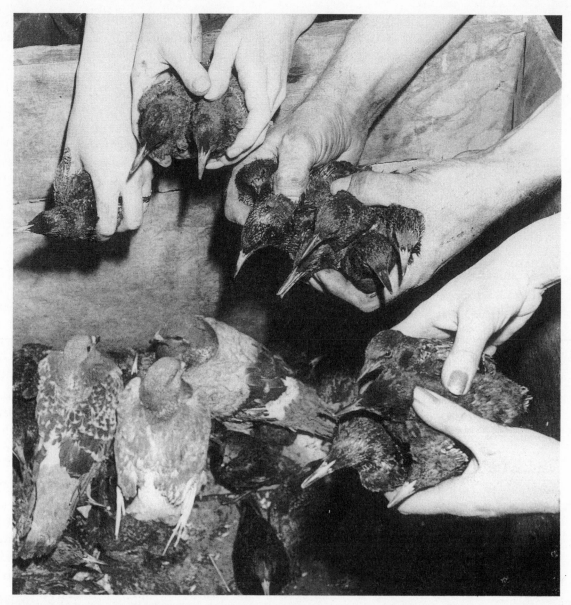

The first wave of casualties rescued before the building was closed

sanctuaries for all species of animal and bird.

I am not a doom-watcher. I have great faith in the voice of reason and, in working at the roots of the countryside on sick, injured or dying wildlife, I see the great surge in people's determination to care for everything living. All over the world the man in the street is being heard and in this country the efforts of bird-gardeners are saving our wild birds. People say that our gardens are the nature reserves of the future. They are wrong. Our gardens are the nature reserves of today!

There are approximately sixteen million gardens in Britain, with the urban sprawl adding more all the time. An estimated one in ten people put out food in some form for wild birds. This probably means there are over 2,500 square kilometres of genuine nature reserves where birds can find food and shelter. And, if we each encourage just one neighbour to design a garden to cater for bird visitors, then there would be 5,000 square kilometres. It's easy, isn't it?

Even the 2,500 square kilometres is far more than those tracts of land sign-posted 'Nature Reserve', where many species are blighted by shooting, culling and other so-called management techniques. Take a look at any one of these nature reserves and notice the lush greenery and waterways. But also notice the lack of anything that moves. Plants and streams cannot walk, jump or fly over the restraining fence into the outside world. They are easy to protect. Birds and other animals demand far more commitment for their protection, and there are still only very few conservation groups *genuinely* looking out for them.

This is where we can play such an important part. Our gardens, large, small, tidy or unkempt, are just lying there crying out to be transformed into ideal bird centres. We can offer attractive fare, desirable residences and all-round protection with little or no effort on our part. There is protection from many of the predators who will not approach man's world, although there is always the scourge of the ubiquitous cat and the occasional blinding slash of speed that is a female sparrow-hawk. A small price to pay for regular food and all those nooks, crannies, mini-cliffs and trees that would make perfect homes.

The seed-eating birds, the finches, sparrows and doves, will collect all those pestering weed seeds blown in on the wind. True, they will also raid the newly sown seedbeds, but as the old rhyme says, when planting seeds:

> One for the pigeon
> One for the crow
> Two to rot and
> One to grow.

And there is the added bonus that the seedlings that do grow will not need thinning out.

There will be berries, fruit and scraps enough to nourish hundreds of birds and then, when this feast is gone, we can help by putting out all manner of foodstuffs, both to help the birds and to provide us with nonstop fascination at their antics, attitudes and often enigmatic intelligence. Already, the British spend over £500,000 a year on wild bird seed, but it is not enough when we realise the benefit in terms of pest control that all these birds will bring to our gardens. If, that is, there are not pesticides and herbicides to maim or kill our visitors. We all know the myriads of bugs, insects, spiders and creepy-crawlies that swarm in our gardens. These are the titbits that attract the non-bird-table birds: the wrens, flycatchers, warblers, thrushes, dunnocks and even the one resident robin.

Just take a look at the menu of a few very familiar garden visitors:

> **The song thrush** will, in a season, take upwards of 10,000 caterpillars, flies, grubs and snails.

> **One pair of great tits** can consume 7–8,000 caterpillars to feed to each brood of youngsters.

> **Blue tits** will decimate aphid populations and even that loveable rogue, **the house sparrow**, will take its fair share of grubs, caterpillars and aphids.

Even in my garden, surrounded with pens of injured sparrowhawks, kestrels and other predators, there is no need to resort to chemicals to control the insect population. Many **dunnocks, robins and blackbirds** brave the icy stares of the birds of prey in their preoccupation with clearing insects. Two resident, one-winged **black-headed gulls** also help by running around all day catching flies and other insects. They are so involved in their pastime that they take no notice of their inability to fly. Sometimes, when I take in a really tiny casualty like a **wren or goldcrest**, then I am often hard pushed to find small insects on which to feed them, and have to resort to buying fruit fly cultures.

As with all forms of conservation and wild animal welfare, Britain still seems to be lagging behind the rest of the world. Even the Americans, with their break-neck life style, manage to devote more time to their garden visitors than we do. And the number of orphaned birds they rescue each spring and take to the hundreds of rescue centres is staggering compared with our few hundred orphans. Our continental cousins in Europe are world-renowned for providing nest platforms on their houses for the largest of all garden birds, the white stork (extinct in Britain).

The redstart, sporadic in Britain, is a common bird on the continent, making use of bizarre nesting sites in France, Switzerland and Belgium that are reminiscent of the odd places favoured by our robin, which I must admit is a shy, woodland bird on mainland Europe. In Germany the black redstart, rare in Britain, is a familiar garden bird known as Hausrotschwanz, the house redtail. With a little effort on our part, I believe that even

The garden bird to beat all garden birds – a rescued gannet

A little auk – another 'first' as a garden bird

these rarities will make the short flight over the North Sea to join the avocet and other wading birds that are re-colonising R S P B reserves.

I do believe, however, that we are gradually improving the situation and turning the tide on our awful record of conservation, although many government agencies still advocate hunting and shooting as the best way to conserve. This abhorrent policy is totally incompatible with my concepts of wildlife protection.

In a survey just after the Second World War, the British Ornithologists Union described 420 species in Britain. This figure had, encouragingly, reached 500 by 1981, with more species nesting than ever before. But before complacency sets in, I think we should realise that this rosy picture is coloured by many new waders and the one-off solitary vagrants blown off course and recorded by 'twitchers', the bird-spotting fanatics who, literally, chase after rarities from one end of Britain to the other.

I believe that every bird, no matter which species, should be given recognition as an individual and not a number. At St Tiggywinkles every bird gets the best of treatment, whether it is a wryneck (a garden species now extinct as a breeding species), or a wren (which statistics tell us is the most populous British bird, with about ten million breeding pairs).

The problem for rarities and twitchers, garden birds and bird watchers, is that many birds are hard to identify positively. So many species have variations. This is especially true of the young birds, and even some of the adults have different colour forms. More difficult still are the newly hatched 'plastics' that have no feathers at all and are often found, blind and helpless, lying on garden paths miles from any nest. We take in dozens of these every year and have to wait until they grow feathers before we can identify them positively. And probably the most difficult, even with all their feathers, are those beautiful little garden songsters, **the warblers**, which remain anonymous at St Tiggywinkles, even after they have been released. I have now mastered most variations, but can still remember myself as a boy, when my identification of birds left a lot to be desired.

I spent my childhood living in Battersea, in south London, just a stone's throw from Clapham Junction. I lived on a small road, a hill that ran down from Lavender Hill. At the top of it was the towering bulk of the local church. Its grounds, surrounded by high, easy-to-climb fencing, contained twelve enormous plane trees, some very sparse grass and a few vagrant shrubs of privet. To us this patch of ground was 'The Woods', our favourite hideout.

My friends and I, our gang, did not have a bird book between us but I could always remember the coloured pictures in the library books. One day, the greyness of 'The Woods' was shattered as I spotted a little, short bird with a long beak and sparkling plumage. Definitely a bee-eater, I thought, the very exotic bird that, on occasions, visits lucky gardens in the south-east of England. This was my first 'tick', an extreme rarity that I watched for hours until my sister spoilt my moment of glory by calling me for tea.

By the following day my bee-eater had flown, so I took the opportunity to go to the library to confirm my find. And there it was on page forty-six of *The Observer's Book of British Birds – Sturnus vulgaris*, a starling. My first 'tick' and first stringer (false claim), to quote birdspotting jargon gleaned from Bill Oddie's *Little Black Bird Book.*

With starling egg on my face I worked every Saturday for ten weeks to afford my own copy of *The Observer's Book of British Birds*. Five shillings well spent. I still have that now-battered little book, with all my scribblings of the time, and I notice that my son Colin recorded his first ticks and finds in the same margins.

Starlings have, since then, always seemed to strut their way into my life. One of the vivid memories of the warehouse that I used before I sold my business and started the wildlife hospital, was of the annual crop of fledgling starlings which would exit their nest in the warehouse roof to play Russian roulette with the cars and feral cats in the car park. I managed to rescue a few but, in my ignorance

of rearing orphan birds, lost most of them. Thankfully, over the last fourteen years since I have been running St Tiggywinkles, I have mastered the problem of orphan starlings and now expect a hundred per cent success rate during 'starling week', when the hospital reverberates to the trilling of dozens of these orphaned, thick-lipped birds.

The centres of our large cities are inhabited by nothing but sparrows and pigeons, along with thousands of starlings commuting from the green lawns of suburbia to take advantage of the cliff-ledge roosting offered by some of our most impressive buildings. Suburbia itself, on the fringes of all our large towns and extending to over 400,000 hectares, offers a never-ending, ever-growing woodland-edge habitat of the type where most species of small bird prefer to live and breed. Even if they are not fed, most birds are welcomed and even entertained in the houses themselves, whereas many mammals, reptiles and amphibians; wood mice, snakes and toads, are treated as vermin, to be killed or, at best, driven out.

This, to me, is another example of the hypocritical double standard that still riddles many people's idea of conservation. I think we are perfectly right to condemn the Mediterranean countries for shooting and trapping our migratory garden birds on their mammoth treks to Africa, but many people in

A cheerful, cocky starling

this country still think it perfectly fair to shoot ducks, waders and other large birds which may well be some other country's migratory birds.

Our garden birds are dear to us and yet they do not belong to us. A lot of them spend many weeks of the year commuting between countries thousands of kilometres apart. Countries all around the world have identical garden birds, although the house sparrow in Rio de Janeiro or the starling in Central Park, New York, are probably descendants of British birds, foolishly released in foreign countries by our misguided Victorian forefathers. Similarly, budgerigars and ring-necked parakeets from tropical countries are now thriving on our bird tables in the south east and also, unfortunately, on the Kent fruit orchards to some extent.

These foreign immigrants aside, a mature British garden can provide maintenance for over sixty species of wild bird, three hundred species of plant and thousands of insects to pollinate these plants and be food for all those birds.

This book is the result of my encounters with thousands of garden birds. Not the birds seen by sitting high on some remote cliff or deep in an isolated marsh, but the birds which live in our world and feature in our lives. The countryside outside the garden is an increasingly barren, hostile environment, devoid of anything alive and moving. We are responsible for that and, in my opinion, owe a great

debt to wildlife, which we can partially repay by offering our gardens for its use.

I am still up to my neck in starlings. Having rescued another 200 from Pitstone, I am learning every intricate detail of the typical garden bird. The story of saving their lives, which has taken many, many hours of delicate care, and has been a major rehabilitation exercise, is covered later in this book.

I have given a brief note on how garden birds have thrust themselves into my life, but on looking back through history, it's easy to see how the people of Britain became involved with garden birds even before they had gardens.

2 Fact, Fiction or Fallacy?

History

Of course, in prehistory, when the first birds evolved, there were no people around to witness their arrival. The earth at that time, around 150 million years ago, was patrolled by gigantic dinosaurs and primitive early mammals, whereas the air buzzed with flying insects – the first form of life to exploit an aerial existence. The pterosaurs, the often gigantic flying reptiles, were also in the air, particularly around the cliffs. We would assume that it made sense for birds to evolve from these pterosaurs but their lineage came to an abrupt halt in the Cretaceous period, approximately fifty million years later.

In fact, we still know very little about the evolution of the first birds. We were always taught that they had evolved from the reptiles but, as always with traditional teaching, once you look closely at previously accepted facts you begin to see flaws and are entitled to seek out your own theories.

Reptiles, as we know them today, are ectothermic (cold-blooded) whereas birds are very much endothermic (warm-blooded), with a body temperature much higher than that of the mammals. Looking at evolution, the far more exciting transition than taking to the air is the bird's ability to generate its own body heat.

Modern day questions are being directed at the whole, accepted rationale on prehistoric animals. For instance: were the dinosaurs in fact warm-blooded reptiles needing the extra, self-generated energy to move their great bulk? There were two types of dinosaur, as we perceive them, the lizard-hipped dinosaur that walked on four legs, and the bird-hipped dinosaur that adopted an upright, kangaroo-like posture, relying on their powerful back legs and, dare I say it, their warm blood, to be fleet of foot both for hunting and for evading capture by larger, carnivorous cousins. The smaller, possibly warm-blooded dinosaurs had all the attributes necessary to evolve into birds.

However, in order to fly, the potential bird would have to have been as light as possible and be capable of expending tremendous energy to stay aloft. Both these criteria for flying had serious consequences for the warmth of the bird's blood. The small size meant that body heat loss would be much faster than in a larger animal and also flying itself would add to the drain on the body warmth. There was only one answer; a light-weight coat that could retain body heat but at the same time not hinder the bird's flying ability, in fact it might even help. The answer was, of course, feathers.

Nobody knows, yet, how feathers evolved, but in 1861 in the soft Jurassic deposits of southern Germany, a fossil reptile was found. It showed the unmistakable impression of a feather. The age of this fossil, about 150 million years, makes it the oldest trace of birds as we know them, even though the crow-sized *Archaeopteryx lithographica*, as the fossil was christened, had a mouth full of teeth, a reptile skeleton (or was it a small, warm-blooded dinosaur skeleton?) and a very small breast-bone, which meant it was very weak at flying.

Following this first bird and over the next seventy million years, the dinosaurs gradually died out, to be replaced by more advanced mammals and newer, more bird-like birds. Some were still so large as to be flightless – the 2-metre long *Hesperornis regalis*, for instance, resembled our present-day divers, even though it still had the vestiges of teeth. Much more familiar and also from the same Creta-ceous chalk of north America as *H. regalis*, was

the 20-centimetre long *Ichthyornis victor*, which was not unlike our present-day terns, although we still don't know if it retained its ancestral teeth, absent in all modern birds.

The only tooth in modern birds is the so-called egg tooth, which grows on the end of the beaks of embryonic birds still in the egg. This egg tooth enables them to break out of the egg. It falls off a few days after hatching.

Mythology

From the end of the late Cretaceous period, about sixty-four million years ago, the fossil records for birds are far more comprehensive, although the first time they are recorded as an integral part of the life of man, other than as food, was only seven thousand years ago, in the mythology of the Sumerian dynasty of south Mesopotamia. But even that distant mythology has been carried down over the generations to affect some of our lives, especially on Boxing Day.

E. A. Armstrong, in his *Folklore of Birds* (Collins 1958) diligently traced the myths back to the Sumerian regime when, it was said, an outlaw bird, Zu, was regularly chased after it had supposedly snatched the destiny-tablet of the gods. The mythology eventually travelled to the British Isles, where Zu was replaced by a wren and the belief compro-mised by making the wren the King of the Birds. Ancient customs dictated that, in order to obtain good fortune, it was necessary to sacrifice your king to the gods while he was

Exactly how birds came to have feathers is still a mystery

still fit and able. I would think that somewhere along the line a particularly wise king decreed that the same positive results could be guaranteed by sacrificing the king of the birds instead. The king of the birds was, and still is, accepted as the eagle, but to capture and then sacrifice this great bird was much more daunting than if the king was a diminutive wren.

So, for many hundreds of years, a crowd would annually chase, capture and often kill a wren, to be borne in glory through the streets to a place of sacrifice. The poor wren would then be trussed or suspended from various poles and be carried by four strong men or two carthorses in a burlesque on its kingship. In the true spirit of sacrifice, its feathers were sometimes plucked and given, individually, to each villager as a talisman for the ensuing year.

The customary chase and sacrifice was usually on, or near, St Stephen's Day, 26 December, or Boxing Day as we know it. Sometimes the wren was roasted; sometimes, if it wasn't killed, it would be set free and sometimes, if no wren was found, then another bird would be hunted and taken. Thankfully, with the changes in attitude towards birds and the bird protection laws, the practice has died out.

For hundreds of years after the Sumerians, birds continued to feature mainly as mythological characters. In particular, the ancient Egyptians focused their attention on the well-known Phoenix and the sacred ibis, a bird which retains its image of sacredness nearly 3,000 years later. The ibis' claim to fame was that, in the formative days of the Egyptian dynasty, it would destroy invading dragons which flew in along the narrow gorge between Arabia and Egypt. So high was the ancient Egyptians' regard for the ibis that they would often deify it with sacrifice and mummification.

The actual natural history of birds did not really get under way until Aristotle (384–322 BC) recorded observations which were not too far removed from the truth. He commented that, 'The cuckoo lays in a nest which she has not built herself, but of some smaller bird, eating the egg there and leaving her own.' Not bad, and even more impressive when you read that as recently as 1899, Saunders wrote that the cuckoo laid on the ground and then carried the egg to the nest. It was not until 1922 that the story of the cuckoo's parasitism was accurately described.

Pliny the Elder (AD 23–79) was renowned for his observations of animal life although, like Aristotle, there were always a few assumptions to plug the gaps in his knowledge. He accurately observed that each cuckoo chooses a particular host and conjectured that the reason for the cuckoo's parasitic life style was that it was hated by all birds and had to lay its eggs anonymously otherwise they would be destroyed by its enemies.

From Pliny onward the story of birds

becomes largely that of the birds which live in close proximity to man – garden birds – and could presumably be studied at close quarters by writers.

Just as today, the three species that appear to dominate literature are the robin, the swallow and the wren. All are highly thought of, unlike poor old sparrow, who has always had a bad press. Even though the Bible tells of God's concern for them, tradition has it that Satan entrusted the guarding of the fires of Hell to a sparrow, who failed dismally when a swallow came down to steal fire for the use of man. The sparrow did, however, manage to tweak some feathers from the centre of the swallow's tail giving it, forever, the familiar fork that easily differentiates it from martins and swifts.

The 'big three', the robin, wren and swallow, have all traditionally helped man in one way or another. In practically every country where they are known, swallows are seen as the harbingers of summer. They were, along with storks, the first birds protected by law. That was by official decree in Milan in 1496. Robins and wrens have always been protected by superstition, although the taboo on wrens was lifted once a year for the wren hunt, and robin redbreast was described as a 'light and good meat' by Thomas Muffet in *Health's Improvement*, published in 1595. I suppose that there are always a few people who will resist tradition. Even today, when most people accept that swans are the property of the Queen, institutions like St John's College, Cambridge still kill and roast 'the royal bird' for their Annual Dinner.

I respect the lives of birds and don't really subscribe to taboos. I have always felt that any bird brought to the wildlife hospital needs help, otherwise it could not have been caught. Some we save and some we are not able to and of these, some are robins. It's horrifying to think that custom says, 'Holding a dying robin may cause trembling and palsy in the hands for the rest of one's life.' I have held a few tiny robins in my hand as they have breathed their last but, thankfully, still have hands steady enough to help the next one that comes in.

Another robin fallacy is that cats will not kill them. Believe me, they do and only last year I was terribly worried because of the vast influx of baby robins caught by cats. The birds that arrive here are the minority so I had serious misgivings about how many were, in fact, being killed.

The tameness of the robin in this country is attributed to the lack of persecution over the centuries. Even Chaucer (1340–1400) remarked on the temerity of 'the tame ruddock (robin)' and there's the story of St Serf and a tame, handfed robin which dates from as long ago as the sixth century. I only hope that these little birds' encounters with cats don't change their attitude, no matter how slowly evolution works.

Apart from the gruesome medical remedies

With time and patience, robins will feed from your hand

that include using the powdered ashes of burnt robin as an ingredient for the removal of bladder stones and epilepsy, the robin has, since the time of the New Testament, been highly regarded; even its faeces were regarded as being useful against stomach upsets, sunburn, scurf or freckles.

As early as Roman times its red breast was attributed to wounds received while trying to pluck thorns from Christ's crown at the Crucifixion. Another red-breast theory is that it was singed while taking refreshing water to sinners in Hell. The well-known 'Babes in the Wood' story is probably an adaptation of Thomas Lumpton's piece of 1579:

A Robbyn readbreast, finding the dead body of a Man or Woman, wyll cover the face of the same with Mosse. And as some holdes opinion, he wyll cover also the whole body.

Folk tales thrive on the subject of robins. Was Robin Hood real or just another robin legend? The story of the killing of cock robin by the poor, maligned sparrow still echoes around our nursery schools. The first printed version of this tale appeared as long ago as 1744; or is the bird which is transfixed by an arrow on a fifteenth-century stained glass window in Buckland Priory, Gloucestershire, a much earlier reference?

Most legends are fairy tales, but reading between the lines of some of them, we can see evidence of sound observation. For instance:

> The north wind doth blow,
> And we shall have snow,
> And what will the robin do then?
> Poor thing.
> *Songs for the Nursery*, 1805

which tells us correctly that snow in England usually comes in on a north wind and that small birds suffer hardship in these conditions.

Literature

Of course, knowledge and history cannot rely entirely on folklore or fairy tales, and as early as in ancient Greek or Roman times, Aristotle and Pliny were attempting textbooks on natural history subjects. The twelfth and thirteenth centuries saw an upsurge in bestiaries, books of beasts. Even though the dragons, unicorns and griffons in the bestiaries harped back to folklore, the descriptions of other creatures were reasonably sound – a step in the right direction.

The first recorded printed bird book *Avium Pracipuarium*, was produced in 1544 at Morpeth, Northumberland, by William Turner. It was a study document, unlike the one written only a few years previously by Polydore Virgil, who had written of the culinary delights of birds.

> The cheefe foode of the Englishman consisteth in flesh –
> Of wilde burdes these are most delicate partriches, pheasaunts, quayles, owsels, thrushes and larks

Possibly Turner's *Avium Pracipuarium* helped identify the reader's next meal.

Sound observation was fast becoming an integral part of writing about birds. Izaak Walton, for instance, broke with the tradition which held that a nightingale's song was melancholy, when he wrote:

> The nightingale breathes such sweet loud music out of her little instrumental throat that it might make mankind to think miracles had not ceased.

But most other writers, especially poets, tended, like the seventeenth-century Richard Barnfield, to see the nightingale as 'a doleful

bird, a female, perpetually lamenting, even leaning its breast against a thorn to make its mourning more poignant'; a reference dating all the way back to the legend of Philomela and Procne, where Tereus cut out the tongue of his wife Procne lest she should disclose his violation of her sister Philomela. Philomela was transformed into the melancholic nightingale, the tongueless Procne became the twittering swallow and Tereus became the hoopoe – all garden birds again. Mind you, the hoopoe is very rare in this country.

Gilbert White (1720–93) was the first natural history writer accepted by modern naturalists. Letters of his observations, subsequently published in 1789, were the solid base from which modern writing has developed. Charles Darwin himself used White's treatise on the earthworm for his own writing in the following century. The disappearance each year, however, of the swallows, swifts and martins always confused him. He knew that the naturalist Morton's statement of 1703, that swallows migrated to the moon, was hopelessly off course. He knew from correspondence with his brother in Gibraltar that they regularly crossed the Straits of Gibraltar going south in the autumn and north in the spring. But he could not fathom out how a newly fledged yearling swallow could make such a journey. He discounted the theory that

There is nothing fictitious about the magpie's thieving tendencies – it is a favourite pastime

they hibernated with frogs in the bottom of pools – which probably originated from their habit of congregating in reed beds before migration. He was convinced they hibernated, but searches of all likely nooks and crannies did not produce one sleeping bird. It was not until regular bird ringing was undertaken earlier this century that the true marvels of migration were fully described and accepted.

However, the mystery of the winter disappearance of the swallow and its regular habit of nesting with man, has made it a central figure in the bird-lore over many centuries. In legend, just like the robin with its red breast, the red patches on a swallow's neck and forehead are attributed to deeds performed for the good of man. Well known as the harbinger of summer on 25 March each year, on the Feast of the Annunciation, the swallows supposedly fly down from paradise to bring warmth to the earth.

Also, in Spain, just like the robin, the redness is put down to the swallow trying to remove the thorns from Christ's crown. In Portugal the redness is attributed to the swallow trying to wipe away Christ's blood. The Russians thought it was as a result of trying to remove Christ's torturing nails, whereas the Swedes think that the swallow's incessant twittering consoled Christ in His torment.

Sharing centre stage in spring is the cuckoo, another bird of mystery and therefore importance. There is still a little nursery rhyme sung in our schools that originated from a long-ago thirteenth-century manuscript. The words may have been changed, understandably, but the springtime elation is still there:

Summer is y-comen'in
Loude sing, cuckoo!
Groweth seed and bloweth mead
And spring'th the woode now:
Sing, cuckoo!

Ewe bleateth after lamb,
Low'th after calfe cow,
Bullock starteth, bucke farteth,
Merry sing, cuckoo!
Cuckoo, cuckoo,
Well singes thou, cuckoo,
Ne swik thou never now.

It all seems that spring is in the air, until you realise that if you heard its first notes from the north then rain and storm would follow. The number of calls told you how long you were to live, or the years of maidenhood left for village girls. If, on hearing the first call, you had money in your pocket, you would have a year of plenty, but an empty pocket meant poverty. If the call came from the right you would be prosperous, from your left meant the opposite, while walking on hard ground meant calamity, and so on. I assume you had to be a contortionist or deaf not to have your life style changed for ever by the call of a bird. And, just to add to your dilemma, the cuckoos' return is unpredictable even though, once again, tradition gives exact dates for when you can expect to hear the first call. The only

ring of truth is that Yorkshiremen expect their cuckoos about a week after the bird's arrival in Sussex.

All these garden birds have figured in village life for centuries. Their names feature highly amongst the names of plants and creatures of the wayside. Cuckoopint and cuckoo spit are probably familiar but what about a cuckoo flower (which we know as lady's smock)? The swallow was believed to collect greater celandine to heal its babies' eyes; in herbal tradition the plant became recommended as the cure for blindness and was known as 'swallow herb'. When the gall wasp lays its eggs in the unopened bud of a wild rose, the ensuing deformity is 'robin's pincushion'. And we've all heard of 'sparrow's kneecaps' and 'pigeon toes', two traditional bird-like descriptions still in use today.

I dread to think what will happen when the new bird nomenclature for Europe is brought in – 'the European robin's pincushion' is really quite a mouthful. Probably the blackbird will become the 'dark thrush' or something similar.

Incidentally, did you know that blackbirds used to be white? They only became black when, during one particularly bad winter in the Brescia region of Italy, a white blackbird took refuge in a chimney and came out black with soot and so it remained. To this day, the

The cuckoo – another bird of mystery. This one is still a fledgling looking for a free meal

last two days of January and the first of February are known as 'blackbird days'.

The twentieth century has seen a more factual alignment with garden birds. As early as the turn of the century, Christmas cards showed four robins and were out of touch with reality because robins are solitary birds. But Christmas cards from then on have shown only one robin.

Garden birds are now very prominent in our lives. They are on coins, stamps, bank notes, and there are even cars named after them. Some of their popularity and the welcome we show them may stem from their visits to the damnable trenches in the battlefields of the Great War (1914–18), when the infantrymen would bet on the bird's chances of survival. I am sure that those men who returned brought with them a closer affinity to birds than there had ever been before.

They were probably the first modern bird gardeners who, when back home, saw with a fresh eye the birds in their gardens and started the ball rolling to provide better habitats for their visitors. Nobody after the 1914–18 War had much money to pay for food for the birds; they could hardly afford to feed themselves and their families. But what they could do was collect natural food from the countryside and store it for the birds. And in their gleaning they might also come across a seedling hawthorn or sycamore that they could transplant into their gardens at no extra cost – the first steps into bird gardening. Mind you, just

before the War, gardeners had dug up all their cotoneasters, which would sometimes attract wintering waxwings to feed on their berries. The reason? The scarlet wing decorations of waxwings made them precursors of war, which had to be discouraged.

There appears to be very little written about the other garden birds, although Shakespeare did mention the dunnock as 'the hedge sparrow' – a nickname that stuck until very recently, when it was proved that it was no relation of the sparrow.

The robin and the blackbird used to be shy woodland birds. It was only when they started to approach man that they figured in his folklore. Perhaps the finches, tits and starlings were also shy woodland birds until the advent of serious bird gardening over the last sixty years, which encouraged them out into the open and on to the trees being planted especially for this purpose.

3 Let It Grow

Gradually, over the centuries, we have become more and more aware of garden birds, both because of their increasing physical presence in our lives and because of the almost imperceptible propaganda in our literature, advertisements and even our cigarette packets. However, the garden birds themselves have probably not yet benefited from the close association and our incursions into their world. Once upon a time, a hard winter meant that small birds had to forage more vigorously to survive, but then there were hundreds, even thousands, of square miles of uncultivated wilderness bursting at the seams with all manner of fruits, berries, nuts, seeds and weeds. These, in turn, were festooned with hibernating, protein-rich insects and grubs – more than ample to sustain even the tiniest birds like wrens, goldcrests and the now extremely rare Dartford warbler through the severest weather.

Nowadays, as man takes more and more of the countryside under his control, there are not the vast tracts of wilderness available for foraging. Small, susceptible birds probably have less than one tenth of the land resources available for possibly the same amount of population, with the addition of the now substantial population of collared doves, the numbers of which, since their first appearance in 1955, have increased dramatically. They, too, now compete for the seed food source. Apart from the competition from the influx of the collared dove, man alone has been responsible for the decimation of the small birds' winter supplies, and now it is man alone who can provide the supplements crucial for the survival of the smaller species, our subject – the garden birds.

Supplying additional food for the birds

Happily, there are five proven methods of providing extra sustenance for visiting garden birds, but all five have one important thing in common: they must all provide a regular supply. Birds are very much creatures of habit and although they probably plan their foraging they can become complacent about the

food available at familiar feeding stations.

The first three methods involve getting supplies of suitable foodstuffs and putting them out regularly on to trays or bird tables – feeding stations. Seed, titbits and various insectivorous foods can be bought from reputable dealers and are ideal for the armchair bird-gardener, although they can be expensive.

A far cheaper method is to approach local organic farmers and ask for the sweepings from their grain stores, or even permission to scour their recently harvested fields for gleanings: the seeds spilled by the harvester that, in Victorian times, sustained much of the poorer population. In fact, not only is it cheaper, but many farmers would also welcome the help in cleaning their stores and fields for the next crop. I would strongly advise sticking to organically farmed seed as there is no telling which chemicals were used with the more regular farming methods. We inevitably take chemicals in with our food but why make the birds suffer the same contamination?

The other 'fresh air' method of gathering feed for the bird stations is to go out into the countryside to collect seeds, berries, fruits and nuts and store them for winter use. I know that this may be tantamount to taking the food from the mouths of wandering, foraging birds that will not visit gardens, but I believe that in the wild many of these goodies go to

The occasional 'yaffle' – green woodpecker – will visit gardens to feed on ants

waste and our ham-fisted incursions will have no detrimental effect on the bands of finches which scour the countryside for thistle, teasel and other seed heads. The amounts we store will be far more effective lifesavers as regular bird-table offerings in the depths of winter.

Gardening to feed the birds

These methods of providing bird-station fare all require regular supplies of foodstuffs and regular, disciplined 'shelf-filling'. The other lazy way of providing some food for garden birds, with absolutely no involvement whatsoever, is simply to let your garden run riot. Never prune a bush or sweep a path or weed a weed. It won't look untidy as nature has a great way of making everything mould into one landscape. However, it might not be very popular with your neighbours and in true Mother Nature tradition will, over the years, revert to scrub and eventually primaeval forest. Not to be recommended for a typical suburban garden but probably a wonderful exercise with about 12 hectares.

The freshly overgrown garden will be a store of seed and invertebrate food for the visiting birds, but it will need managing eventually and, after all, with proper management and judicious pruning, the crop of seed yield can be multiplied threefold.

Although an overgrown garden is attractive, it is not my ideal of an oasis for wildlife. I am by nature a latent gardener and before embarking on building up the Wildlife Hospital Trust, spent many years experimenting with various garden plants to suit all manner of purposes. Now my ideal bird garden is one planted with a complete range of trees, shrubs, herbaceous plants and grasses that will provide a larder of fresh food for the garden's visitors. Not only can this garden be attractive, lucrative and rewarding, its concept and management can be exciting, as you try out new plant species, and challenging, as you produce newcomers from cuttings and seeds begged, borrowed, but preferably not stolen from other gardens.

In my late teens, for some unknown reason, I had this yen to start gardening. Rather than splash out with some of my £2.10s. a week that I earned as an articled accountant, I took to getting cuttings and seeds from uncles and aunts. I even built myself a small greenhouse above the coal cellar, with glazed window frames from a demolition site. It was about this time that I first met Sue, who still reminds me of our early courting days spent tenderly nurturing cuttings and elephants' feet cacti in my 'greenhouse'.

It was during these years of discovering plants that I learnt how simple twig or leaf cuttings could soon be transformed from one plant into dozens. I used to walk Sue home to Chelsea via the manufactured glades of Battersea Park. Many of my prime specimens started life as surreptitiously broken-off twig cuttings, pocketed before the brown-coated park keepers spotted our diversions.

Now that I have more appreciation of the glades created in city centres by parks like Battersea, I would no doubt frown on anybody damaging any plant trying to survive, especially in central London. However, with permission and care, there are numerous cuttings to be had from friends' gardens and even from the plant nurseries at the centre of all council-run parks and recreation grounds, where a few planting tips from the groundsmen/gardeners are always an added bonus.

Planting your garden: Large trees

In those unenlightened days, nearly all London gardens were bounded by blank, dark privet or laurel bushes, which offered nothing to birds to eat except the occasional looper caterpillar. With the vast choice available to gardeners these days it's possible to plan a planting programme that will provide natural food – seeds, berries and invertebrates – throughout the colder months every year without the necessity of remembering to fill or clean a bird table regularly. Usually the cold months only stretch from January to March, but even with those occasional, long November to April winters, your natural store should see most birds through, although it may be necessary to supplement with a little bought seed and fruit during really frozen spells when 'every bird and its mother' will flock to your winter larder.

When it actually comes to the choice of plants for the garden, there is a crusade at the

Orphaned wrens pose a particularly difficult feeding problem

moment which stresses that every planting should be of an indigenous species. That's all very well if you are re-creating a lost landscape, but we are trying to plant specifically to service the bird population. The aesthetics are an important but secondary consideration. To obtain the best for the birds, ignore the indigenous lobby and their smoke-screens and look to the bounty some introduced species will provide.

Unfortunately, nobody bothered to tell the birds that they are supposed to feed only on indigenous species. No doubt they have seen the propaganda that the English oak is second to none, with a staggering 300-plus species of insects reliant on its broad body. Nobody,

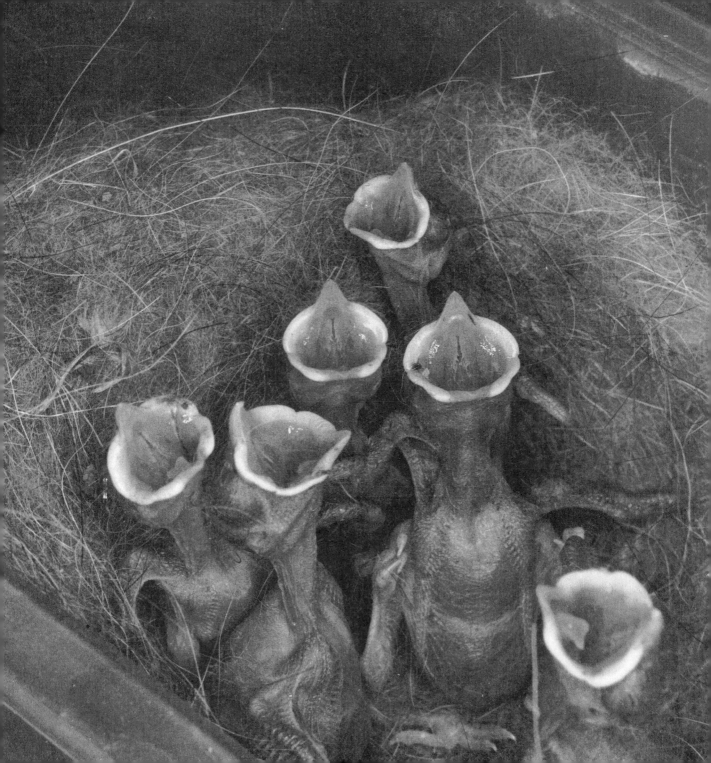

however, seems to mention that most of these insects are probably bitter or tasteless and only taken as a last resort. Much better, if you are a bird, to feast on the myriad of succulent aphids which swarm on that arch-alien, **the sycamore**, which after all has grown in Britain for only 500 years.

Recently Kirsi Peck of the University of Durham studied, on a Forestry Commission planting of conifer and broad-leaved woodland, the feeding behaviour of six species of bird – blue tit, great tit, coal tit, chaffinch, goldcrest and tree creeper – six of our most valued garden birds. Top of the list of trees and clearly preferred by all six species was, you've guessed it, the sycamore, and way down the list were those British stalwarts the oak, beech and ash. Bottom of the 'tit parade' was the bleak, cold Norway spruce.

Even with this track record, most conservationists still treat sycamore as undesirable aliens. Many conservation volunteers are told to pull up the prolific sycamore seedlings on sight. In fact, this practice is probably contrary to the provisions of the Wildlife and Countryside Act 1981, which states that: 'Any person who, not being an authorised person, intentionally uproots any wild plant shall be guilty of an offence.' We are told that 'sycamore is a weed', but then isn't every plant that does not feature in a nurseryman's catalogue?

Baby birds don't know what 'indigenous plant' means – they will eat anything their mother brings

To me, it seems a great pity and perhaps folly that the Forestry Commission, who want quick-growing softwood, plant millions of acres of black, barren conifer forest which suppresses wildlife, whereas sycamore would grow just as quickly, be far more pleasant to look at and walk through, and would allow light to reach the forest for ground-hugging plants like violets, aconites and even bluebells. To top this impressive list of benefits sycamore would also provide plenty of live insects for parent birds to feed to their young, apart from sustaining bees and dormice.

But purists need not despair. There are small British trees, not with the pedigree of the mighty oak, but with a prolific growth rate just like the sycamore, which will enable you to see a mature tree in your lifetime, not 200 years later.

Probably the prettiest and most useful British tree is the very graceful **silver birch**. In fact, the Forestry Commission are actually looking to this tree to replace the spruce forests. Silver birch is easily available from nurserymen, is quick to grow, has a resident population of tasty insects and also produces catkins of seeds to suit the harder-billed birds. To top all this, it dies quite young, but as it decays it produces even more insects and attracts woodpeckers and treecreepers, providing them, starlings, nuthatches and some of the tits, with easily excavated nest sites.

In many of our aviaries at the hospital we grow several **white willow**, *Salix alba*, all of

The rare wryneck, camouflaged in its natural, wooded environment

birds pecking at the myriads of tiny insects on each long thin leaf. To add to this, just like the birch, each willow produces masses of protein-laden catkins. Just a little note of caution: willows have very invasive root systems and should not be encouraged near to houses or other buildings.

There are, of course, many other species of large tree, but most take an age to reach any size and if you are as impatient as I am you will want to see substantial growth not too long after planting. The three trees I have mentioned; the sycamore, birch and willow, will give a quick return on your invested effort and will provide a much richer food source than most other species.

Planting your garden: Smaller trees and shrubs

In a true forest ecosystem there are various layers of plant growth exploited by various species of bird and insect. The larger trees would be the forest canopy, then just below them would be the shrubby trees which often produce crops of berries to tempt birds to feed. It's often in the latter's interest to have birds take their offerings; a seed which has passed through a bird's digestive system is far more likely to germinate successfully.

A very graceful tree that produces its bright, succulent berries earlier than any other shrub is the **rowan**, or **mountain ash** as it is sometimes known. So popular are the rowan fruit that bird catchers once used them

which grew from one twig literally stuck in the ground. Their growth rate is phenomenal, with us having to cut them back every year or else, in 15–20 years, they would grow to 25 metres or more. All the prunings are also stuck in the ground and within a year have become healthy small trees. Even in our garden under the gaze of sparrowhawks and kestrels, the willows are always full of small

The hazards of nesting in a thorn bush

as bait to snare thrushes, redwings and field-fares, which find them irresistible. As I say, rowans are early fruiters and their branches are often stripped before other shrubs have their berries ripe and ready for eating. However, rowan berries can be lifesavers to nourish redwings, fieldfares and other migra-tory thrushes when they first arrive in the autumn after flying all the way from Scandi-navia. Also, strictly insectivorous birds such as the flycatcher and wren will avail them-selves of the rowan's early harvest, especially in cool weather when many insects are snugly hidden out of the way.

Cherries are the other trees that produce clusters of rich, succulent fruit. So popular are the *Prunus* family that the French plant wild cherries, *Prunus avium*, around their orchards in order to deflect the, often minimal, damage to their fruit trees by blackbirds and thrushes. Just why *Prunus avium* (meaning 'bird') should be the 'wild cherry' and *P. padus* be the 'bird cherry' is anybody's guess. However, the bird cherry is favoured by birds for its bitter fruit,

In the winter, these berries will disappear in no time

its unpalatability making them safe from the ravages of scrumping by small boys. The spring buds are highly favoured by bullfinches, so in fruit-growing areas extra plantings of *P. padus* would distract many of those handsome birds, rendering them less liable to persecution by fruit farmers.

Similarly, purging **blackthorn**, a natural in any traditional hedge, is much favoured by bullfinches for its buds in January and February and its round, black berries on the female trees in August. Its name is derived from the drastic purgative which used to be made from its bark and berries. However, this doesn't seem to bother the caterpillars of the gorgeous brimstone butterfly and dark umber moth, which prefer **buckthorn** as their main food plant.

Thorn bushes are very important to birds, both for the berries they supply and for the nest sites that offer the greatest protection. And the queen of all thorns – and luckily for bird gardeners, the commonest and easiest to propagate and grow – is the **hawthorn**. Its glorious blossom, in May and June, stimulated many ancient festivals and fertility rites. The species list that nest in hawthorn is only outnumbered by the list of those that feed on the clusters of haws in the autumn. Beware, though, for the ornamental, double-flowered varieties sold by many nurserymen do not produce berries.

The sheer versatility of hawthorn makes its presence in any garden an absolute must. For a start, it's easily grown from the many seedlings to be found around established bushes, but do remember the law about uprooting wild plants. Get your seedlings from a friend's garden.

Once established, hawthorn can be grown as an impenetrable hedge – that is, impenetrable by all but the nesting birds. It will need trimming and possibly layering during the winter, but if left to grow it will soon make a small tree about 3.5 metres high, which will still be nested in by birds and have that added bonus of May blossom and masses of autumn haws. It will also grow very quickly, especially if it is pruned regularly to produce thick growth low down on the trunk. A tree or shrub that is not restricted in its first few years may well end up as a tall, bare trunk with a clump of foliage on the top, a situation detested by nesting birds. This applies to most species of shrub, especially fast growers.

With berry-bearing shrubs and fruit-bearing trees, do leave any uneaten fruit to hang for the winter. This will encourage insects, providing, if you like, a second bite of the cherry later when the real cold weather hits.

The only benefit missing from this list of small trees and large shrubs is an evergreen that will provide dry, winter roost sites for the thrush-size birds that would find it difficult to roost in evergreen climbers, the favourite of small birds like wrens and sparrows. The **holly** provides winter dormitories for many birds as well as ample nest sites in spring, as long as thick growth is encouraged by regular clipping. Holly berries are very erratic as a source of bird food and are often only taken as a last resort. It is during the sudden cold snaps later in the winter, when all the other trees and bushes have already been stripped, that the reserve of holly berries can save so many birds' lives. There has to be a male plant and a female plant to cross-pollinate the flowers. However, horticultural genetic engineering is well advanced and your nurseryman will be able to recommend a good species which will produce berries every year. The only drawback with holly is that it is slow-growing, so it may be worth buying a well-grown specimen for planting. One bush, if it is a self-pollinator, should provide good roosting, nesting and a supply of berries both for the birds and for Christmas decorations.

Once the vanguard of trees and shrubs are planted around the garden, it is better to be patient and wait a year or two until they are established before proceeding with the next stage of the mini-forest ecosystem we are trying to reproduce in our suburban 'woodland edge'.

After two years you will be able to see any gaps forming in your planting layout. I know it will make many people gasp, but I would plug these gaps with that great 'weed', the **elderberry**. It grows anywhere and more rapidly than most other species. Its great claim to fame is its regular production of great clumps of rich, dark elderberries, which the birds love. Look under any starling or thrush roost in the autumn and notice the dark purple droppings where the birds have been feasting on the elderberry bounty. I have an elderberry in one of the aviaries and when it grows through the wire netting it provides me with a continual source of aphids for the tiny casualties like wrens and goldcrests, which find any other live food too large for their tiny beaks.

Elderberry will grow on a rubbish tip, or behind a shed. In fact, it will grow anywhere. It's reasonably good for nesting in and when large, its hollow trunks are used by tits and tree sparrows. To top all these attributes, elderflower and elderberry wine are two of the best do-it-yourself vintages. Cut the elder-berry back every year and it will grow more prolifically and produce more than enough for everyone, birds and viticulturists alike – and still form a dense hedge if trained properly.

Planting your garden: Hedges

Hedges should be established from the very first day, not only as nesting and feeding sites, but also as security to keep out unwanted four-legged visitors. I have mentioned **hawthorn** and **elderberry hedges**. **Holly** can be grown as a hedge but is rather slow, just like the traditional **box** or **yew hedges**, which proliferate at about an inch a year. We really want faster growing, more productive hedges like the **hawthorn** and **elder**. One of my favourites, because it keeps its dead leaves as cover during the winter, is the **beech** hedge. The tall, majestic beech tree may have limited benefits for birds, but the dense hedge provides ample nest sites and good cover for winter roosting. It will not provide beech mast like the trees, but then I always think that beech mast is over-rated as a bird food, being far more suited to wild mammals.

The old, bland privet hedges that I know so well from London don't have much use in bird gardening. Instead, if you have the space, I would recommend that you approach a specialist nurseryman and ask for a **Saxon hedge mix of 'whips' and small standards**. We have just planted on the site of the new

A starling with his breakfast

Hospital a hedge which, when it grows, will produce a truly indigenous mix for nesting, roosting and feeding sites, together with the mass of flowers associated with British hedgerows. These specialist nurseries will also advise on soil types, planting and a species mix that is likely to thrive in your area. Wherever you are, add a few briars of **bramble** to all hedges. Apart from the wealth of flowers and blackberries, the thorns add to the security of nest sites. Blackberries are not the greatest of favourites with birds but bullfinches find them tasty. The **thornless Oregon blackberry**, however, is a great favourite of most warblers and finches.

Hedges need very little maintenance other than an annual trimming, well outside the nesting season. In the first few years a systematic pruning will encourage growth right down to ground level. In fact if the hedge is trimmed in an 'A' shape, water and light can get to the wider, lower growth, producing good sturdy platforms for the low-nesting birds like warblers and robins.

Planting your garden: Small shrubs

After the first two years, your hedges and trees should be taking shape and it's time to introduce the next variety of plants to fit into your ecosystem, which by now would be recognised by many birds as their preferred 'woodland edge' habitat. To complete the tier system, you will need smaller shrubs fronted by herbaceous and annual borders, which will provide a wealth of seeds every year, both for the birds and for storing and replanting the following year.

The smaller shrubs may produce nest sites, but their main purpose is to produce all sorts of berries at different times of the autumn and winter. They should be planted about one metre apart and be trimmed back hard to produce dense, low growth. With the larger trees and shrubs it was essential that light was allowed to penetrate through to the lower species, now it is advisable to let the smaller shrubs grow thickly to cut out light to the ground and so discourage invasive plant species that may compete with the preferred shrubs. Because of this, all new plantings should be mulched to a depth of two or three inches; shredded bark mulch is available quite cheaply from most garden centres. Peat used to be the material of choice for mulching but because of the inroads that peat digging has made into many wild, ecologically sensitive areas, its use should be discouraged.

The range of small to medium-sized shrubs is tremendous. If planting to attract birds, it is necessary to seek out those that produce berries or seeds. Overall, they are probably not ideal for nesting in unless one of the smaller finches takes a fancy to a young **dogwood**. Otherwise known as the 'dog tree' or 'dog berry' because its fruit was not even fit for dogs, *Cornus sanguinea* can grow to 4 metres high but can also be kept within bounds by annual pruning. This species has greenish-white flowers, the unpleasant smell of which attracts insects, which in turn attract birds. A further bonus is that the caterpillars of the green hairstreak butterfly feed on the leaves.

The close relative of the dogwood, the **Cornelian cherry**, *Cornus mas*, can grow 7.5 metres high but can also be kept within bounds as a low shrub. It has yellow flowers and far more palatable, red cherry-like berries that are favoured by many species of garden bird.

Both these dogwoods are classed as pure indigenous species, but when we move on to the **barberries**, there is a mixture, from the true native *Berberis vulgaris* through hybrids to cultivars like *atropurpurea*, which has highly coloured foliage. *B. darwinii* and *B. hookeri* are both evergreen, providing good roosting and nest sites together with highly palatable berries in the autumn, which are freely taken by blackcaps, fieldfares and hawfinches. If you are really lucky, then in a 'waxwing year' (the periodic winter eruption when more than the normal number of waxwings journey southeast from their Scandinavian breeding grounds) you may have a fleeting visit from a wandering group of these exotic migrants.

Two indigenous **viburnums** are great favourites of all berry-eating birds. For once the generic name is probably as well known as the English names: the Wayfaring tree, *V. lantana*, and the Guelder rose, *V. opulus*. In the countryside they grow in quite different locations, giving the gardener a choice of *V. lantana*, which naturally grows on well-drained chalk or limestone soils, whereas the original name of the *V. opulus*, the swamp elder, aptly describes its preference for wet soils. Both species produce prolific umbellifers of insect-laden flowers, followed by berries readily eaten by thrushes and waxwings, if they come.

The other viburnun cultivar, the Snowberry bush, is sterile and of no real purpose in the bird garden.

Planting your garden: Herbaceous border

In front of these shrubs and bordering on the manicured lawn, which will be a favourite feeding place of blackbirds, thrushes and starlings, is the herbaceous border. This can be planted up with seed-producing plants, either perennials, biennials or annuals. Any perennials can be left to run to seed before being clipped or tidied up.

Lavender, for instance, is a great favourite of chaffinches, but can grow rather large and should be kept under control, as should **Michaelmas daisies**, the seeds of which are great favourites with many finches.

Tall-growing perennials are **achillea**, with its large, flat heads of brilliant, golden-yellow flowers followed by good seed heads in October. Achillea seeds are ideal for storage and use as bird-table fodder later in the winter. In fact, most of these seeding plants can have excess seeds stored for later use, and of course

Flowers to Attract Birds and Insects

Petunia	Lobelia	Scabious
Valerian	Foxglove	Michaelmas
Thyme	Teasel	daisy
Cosmos	Nettles	Godetia
Marjoram	Chickweed	Honesty
Larkspur	Dock	Sunflower
Evening	Plantain	Delphinium
primrose	Candytuft	Dandelions
Primrose	Lavender	Cornflower
Snapdragon	Night scented	Globe thistle
Aubretia	stock	Forget-me-
Wallflower	Pinks	not

annuals such as **cornflowers, cosmos, gaillardia, godetia, linum, marigold** and **sunflower** – all great favourites with the finches – will need seed taken for the following year's planting.

Some of these can also be treated as perennial, but can be erratic in growing the following year. The marigolds are particularly worth planting for their renown at destroying many soil pests, especially when planted around tomatoes.

Seed should also be taken off the biennials, like the majestic **teasel**, which acts like a magnet to those charmers, the goldfinches. The other must for goldfinches is the rather invasive **thistle**, which produces irresistible crowns of feathery seeds that are absolutely ideal for the goldfinch's rather slender beak.

Although related to goldfinches, and to my mind they are just as handsome, the bullfinches have a very short, stubby beak, ideal for picking seeds off **antirrhinums** and **delphiniums**, two more perennials that need more care in controlling their spread than in cultivating them.

There are many different beak types in the finch family, each evolved for a different job. The goldfinch has a thin beak for probing into teasels and thistles, the hawfinch can crack a nut with one crush of his enormous beak, whereas the crossbill has a peculiar arrangement which enables it to open pine cones and extract the seeds. In fact, it was the variety of beaks on Galapagos finches that first set Charles Darwin off on his *Origin of Species*.

Other small perennials that will produce seeds to please all the finch family, not to mention a showy sward in the garden, are the **forget-me-nots** and **pansies**.

Planting your garden: Weeds

There are other seed producers that used to make gardeners wring their hands in horror and which are still classed as weeds, but which are also proving themselves to be invaluable food plants for many types of animal. **Nettles** are a classic example. A few years ago, to be a nettle meant being pulled up and burnt. Now, as a food plant for many butterfly species, the 'nouveau conservationists' are extolling its virtues as though nobody had ever thought of it.

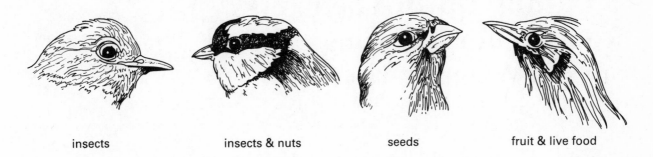

| insects | insects & nuts | seeds | fruit & live food |

Various types of beak evolved for different feeding methods

I know people frown at me because I protect **dandelions**. (In fact, at the new hospital I intend to have a cold greenhouse just to grow the 'yellow peril'. And why? Because I have found it to be the preferred food plant of orphaned rabbits, hares and deer. It succeeds where all artificial diets fail dismally.) Grown in a wild part of the garden, if you can spare the space, you may well see those dainty goldfinches swinging on the stems, delicately picking seeds from the dandelion 'clocks'.

Why not let one part of the garden, even the compost heap run riot with wild seed producers? Apart from the dandelion, there is **chickweed**, another great favourite of mammals and birds when it is in seed. Other so-called weeds are manna to many birds – **dock**, good for nettle stings, invites visits by goldfinches, bullfinches, greenfinches and, in open gardens, that great little songster, the linnet. These four seed-eating birds thrive on the small seeds of the commoner weeds, not just dandelion, chickweed and dock but also **groundsel, shepherd's purse** and, dare I say it, **plantain**.

This chapter has shown just a few of the easy-to-grow plants that may attract garden birds. More than that, just a few of them may, in a bad winter, mean the difference between life and death, especially amongst the smaller birds.

Yet no garden, whether designed for birds or not, can be complete without some of the exciting climbers, and that other essential for all birds and animal visitors, the garden pond. These two features can be created with just a few pots and a plastic liner but their importance and potential to complete the garden demand that they warrant a large part of the next chapter.

4 **Putting Down Their Roots** Natural Nesting Sites & Watering Holes

Many of the fruit and seed-bearing plants I have mentioned will be used for nest sites. Nobody has yet perfected the art of being able to predict where a bird will build a nest. Of course, there are exceptions such as swifts, house martins and swallows, who return to their previous nest sites year after year. This may seem labour-saving, but repeated use of a nest site also gives parasites time to procreate in the nest material, instinctively knowing that a host will return the next season.

You can try to attract other birds to nest by planting potentially suitable shrubs, hedges and climbers, or by pruning existing trees to provide suitable nest platforms.

The best nest position is at the junction of a branch growing at about a 70° angle to the trunk or another sturdy branch. Angles above or below this size will probably prove unsuitable, but always remember that birds are masters of the unexpected and an occasional master builder will probably prove me wrong. As with all bird-nesting projects, never take anything for granted.

Even if a branch *looks* suitable and irresistible to a nesting bird, it may fall short of being a desirable building site. Imagine the questions a bird poses itself before moving in: Is the site sheltered and secluded? Is it too dark or hard to reach? (Remember that woodland birds will only build at the woodland edge, they never nest in the dark interior.) Is there likely to be interference, not just by enemies but from friendly, inquisitive humans? Is there an abundant supply of food?

All these criteria are considered instinctively by the bird choosing the site, usually the female of a pair. Male wrens, in fact, build several 'cock' nest sites, which the female inspects before selecting the most suitable. She then lines it with feathers.

It seems that even a cock wren does not understand the fickleness of a nesting hen, so you might wonder what chance *we* have of predicting a nest site. Not much, but if we adopt the cock wren's behaviour and provide numerous choices, there is more likelihood that there will be *one* des. res. among them.

Dead trees

It is possible to meet all the conditions demanded by a nesting bird in a garden. Obviously, if there is an old, dead tree, riddled with holes, this should be left as a good provider of insect food and as a likely nest site for woodpeckers, nuthatches, tits and, of course, starlings. The one bonus from the major loss of trees to the storms of recent years is the mass of dead or decaying timber nourishing the wildlife food chain. True, there are now gaps in the tree canopy, but isn't this a natural progression? In the original primaeval forest, old and weak trees were culled by the wind in order to encourage new strong plants. Perhaps Britain's tree management programme has been a bit complacent in not replacing old trees before nature showed us how.

Pruning

In the garden, there may already be free-standing trees or shrubs, which can be pruned to provide possible nest sites. There is usually a crown at the top of the tree trunk, from which branches spread to give the tree its shape. If there are three or more branches, then there may be no platform on which a bird can build. By cutting out some of the branches, probably only one or two, a nest site can be fashioned which may attract some of the thrushes, if low enough, or the mistle thrush if it is over 6 metres above the ground.

Similarly, in a smaller bush or shrub, pruning the crown may produce more growth which, after two years, will provide the type of secure nesting site preferred by the most supreme of all the British nest-builders, the chaffinch.

It takes a very bold bird, such as the mistle thrush, to nest in the exposed fork of a tree. Most garden visitors prefer the security and comparatively draught-proof conditions provided by nesting against a wall in one of the many climbing plants. In fact, even outside the nest season, many small birds – wrens, robins and tits – will take to climbing plants for safe, warm roosting.

Climbing plants

Climbers are remarkably fast growers and can be used to cover all manner of structures, from that eyesore of a garden shed to the

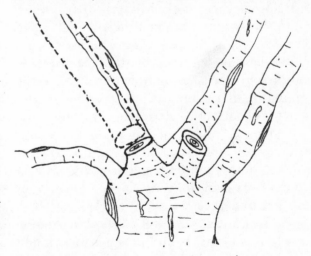

The central branches of a tree removed to provide a good nest site

elegant pergola or arbour, sheltering paths and seats respectively. Light, softwood timber can be bought very cheaply, protected with a *safe* water-based preservative containing no toxic chemicals and initially used to make trellis work that can be fixed to walls and fences to provide a good climbing frame for all manner of climbers. Very simple to make out of 2.5 × 1.25 cm laths mounted on 5 × 5 cm supports, the gaps between the timber can be set at 15 cm by using a piece of old floorboard as a template. Rather than mounting your trellis directly to the wall, mount it on blocks, leaving a gap behind where the plants can grow and where many birds, such as blackbirds, will choose to make their nests.

Pergolas and arbours need to be constructed of more substantial timber, still with a rustic look, or more lasting, 'sawn' timber than that which has been pre-planed. Train climbing plants to cover all your timber structures then, once they are established, blackbirds and thrushes will nest amongst the plants, whilst greenfinches and spotted flycatchers more often than not will choose the flat areas on top of the timber or brick supports. (Any brick supports should be at least 23 cm square and built only six courses at a time. The delays prevent the wet mortar collapsing under the weight of bricks.)

With the vast selection of climbing plants available, there is bound to be one to suit any situation. Take, for instance, that cold, north-facing wall where nothing grows. This is the domain of the **firethorn** *Pyracantha atalantioides*, whose thorny evergreen covering will be used by blackbirds and flycatchers and is an ideal situation for an open-fronted nest box to suit a robin. Firethorn will cover the wall up to 6 metres above the ground; produces masses of white flowers, favoured by bees and other insects, then in September a good crop of berries, so popular that they will all be eaten before the winter takes hold. This plant actually hates a warm, sunny position and will thrive on hard frosts.

The other evergreen which will grow well against a house without damaging the brickwork is the **ivy**, *Hedera helix*. It will, however, cause problems on paintwork, window frames, gutters and eaves. But in spite of this it is a must if you wish to service your bird population. Just take a look at the species that will nest in ivy: starlings, sparrows, blackbirds, robins, flycatchers, wrens, wagtails, blackcaps, wood pigeons, turtle, collared and stock doves, thrushes and chaffinches. I have tried to keep away from lists but the sheer volume of ivy nesters makes it impossible to give the plant due credit any other way.

To add to its nesting attributes, native ivy will produce berries in May and June when other plants are merely flowering. Once established, it can be clipped and kept within bounds just once a year. However, when grown over a dead tree or stump it can be left to run riot, soon producing a green pillar full of invitations to the local bird population.

And how attractive ivy looks growing over old buildings and ruins and over old sheds – nature's own way of beautifying dereliction. What's more, did you realise that it has magical properties which, together with the holly and its Christmas berries, keep the 'house goblin' subdued, especially between Christmas Eve (when the decorations go up) and Candlemas Eve (when they come down)? A tradition obviously based on mythology itself rather than on fact, similar to the fallacy which suggests that ivy growing over a live tree will kill it. It will not do so unless it is allowed to cover the crown completely.

Honeysuckle, on the other hand, has no bad reputation to combat. Quite the opposite, for its powerful evening scent makes it highly desirable in any garden. There are honeysuckles to suit almost every situation. *Lonicera nitida* is an evergreen ideally suited to growing up trellis or, like ivy, over old sheds or tree stumps. Cut any new growth back by about fifty per cent each year and your honeysuckle could well be the nest site of dunnocks, warblers, spotted flycatchers and – if in a remote spot – it may be used by linnets.

Other species such as *L. tragophylla* may be better climbers but all honeysuckles produce juicy berries taken not just by those renowned fruit eaters, the bullfinches, but also by the delicate insect eaters, blackcaps and garden warblers. Pied flycatchers use shredded honeysuckle bark in their nest boxes, as do the now scarce common dormice. As with most

Food from Shrubs		
Hawthorn	Dogwood	Elder
Climbing roses	Firethorn	Ivy
	Honeysuckle	Barberry
Cotoneaster	Wayfaring tree	Buckthorn
Cherries		Crab apples
Holly	Guelder rose	
Rowan	Yew	

climbers, honeysuckle can be propagated by cuttings, that is, a growing branch pulled (*not* cut) from the parent plant. The heel should be trimmed and dipped in a rooting compound powder before being inserted in a small pot filled with damp sand. The whole thing should then be sealed in a polythene bag. As soon as roots are formed the new plant should be re-potted into John Innes No. 1 compost and grown on in a cold frame or greenhouse.

The other classic way of propagating climbers is by layering. Take any shoot that is growing near to ground level. Twist it and push the twist into the ground, holding it in with a peg or bend of wire. Where the twist restricts the flow of sap, the plant will put down roots, forming another plant which can be cut from its parent and planted elsewhere.

Some climbers have a restricted use as nesting sites but the sheer profusion of their berries make them a must in any bird garden. The **cotoneasters** are typical examples, re-

The Russian vine in full flower

quiring clipping for even blackbirds and thrushes to be able to nest. However, during the summer their attractiveness to bees and insects regularly puts them on the insectivorous birds' itinerary and their orange berries are eagerly taken by blackbirds, thrushes, fieldfares, redwings and the ever glamorous waxwings.

Cotoneaster buxifolia, lactea and *franchetii* are evergreen wall plants which give good protection during severe weather. *C. horizontalis* is deciduous but makes up for it with an extraordinary crop of berries. Like most of the climbers, cotoneasters can be trained as hedge plants, giving more scope in nesting for dunnocks and other small birds.

To most people, climbing plants mean **clematis** and their wonderful, plate-sized blooms. Unfortunately, the glamour varieties, those which need pruning, are not much good for anything other than decoration. But there are clematis suitable not just for wall cover but for nest sites. Probably the most popular is *Clematis montana*, which has thousands of small, white, star-shaped flowers in May and June. It can be grown up trellis work or over arches, pergolas and arbours, providing good nest sites for smaller birds such as wrens and goldfinches.

Other suitable species of clematis include evergreen varieties for low, warm walls – *C. armandii* and *C. cirrhosa* – and another rampant climber similar to montana, *C. tangutica*, which has yellow flowers from June to August. The native clematis is *C. vitalba*. Common in most hedgerows, especially in the winter, this is the one known as 'Old Man's Beard'. Unfortunately, it is of little use in the bird garden, although the hollow stems apparently made good tobacco pipes for boys and gypsies; hence other popular names such as 'Boys Bacca', Gypsy's Bacca' and even 'Shepherd's Delight'.

Many species of climber can be grown for their showy flowers with the spin-off that they can also be good nest sites. The really dramatic *Wistaria sinensis*, with its enormous racemes of blue flowers, is the classic climber for 'chocolate box' cottages. It grows to an enormous size and can become a nuisance unless any new growing tips are pinched out in July, after flowering, and also in December. Probably not a good recommendation is the attraction the flowering shoots hold for sparrows.

Apart from that, the **wistaria**'s thick woody branches provide perfect nest sites for blackbirds, thrushes, wagtails, spotted flycatchers.

It's strange how sparrows are attracted to some flowers. In the case of wistaria, the attraction is the blue, and we all know how they like to peck yellow crocuses to shreds. In the case of the **Russian vine**, *Polygonum baldschuanicum*, it seems to be its white flowers that attract. The Russian vine, otherwise known as 'Mile-a-minute' lives up to its nickname and grows up to 2.5 metres in a year. This is the climber to plant if you want to cover walls, sheds, dead trees and eyesores quickly. Just like some of the climbing roses, it needs support and will grow better if it is threaded through trellis work. If you want to cover an eyesore, lay down a framework with large-gauge wire mesh which the Russian vine can clamber over. This will also allow garden birds access for nesting.

At St Tiggywinkles, we make use of a Russian vine to cover four aviaries and it still has to be cut back at least four times a year. To add to this, the plant is actually in our neighbour's garden, yet we get the benefit of this most prolific of the climbers! Garden birds that have availed themselves of Russian vine hospitality include blackbirds, thrushes, dunnocks, linnets, greenfinches, robins and wrens.

The well-known **Virginia creeper**, *Parthenocissus*, fixes itself to a wall by throwing out small discs. It looks very elegant covering the complete side of a house but its value as a source of nest sites is doubtful and, unlike ivy, it can damage brickwork.

Over our original St Tiggywinkles hedgehog unit there grows a prolific **Passion flower**, *Passiflora caerulea*, which started life as a cutting in my father's greenhouse. In a warm, sheltered position, *Passiflora* can be made to spread by giving its roots plenty of space. Alternatively, it can be made to flower more readily by confining its roots before planting.

The passion flower likes a warm, south-facing wall to do really well. If you have such a south-facing situation, it would also be worth trying out some of the more tender climbers like **Ceanothus**, which can flower throughout the whole twelve months of the year, and in towns has a reputation of being tolerant of soot deposits. The **Californian buttercup**, *Fremontodendron californicum*, will relish a south wall and will produce golden flowers from early June until the end of the summer. It also retains its leaves in most winters, providing good evergreen roosting sites for resident birds. All three climbers are readily adopted for nesting by the usual blackbirds, thrushes and robins, together with wagtails and flycatchers.

The other well-known climbers, the **jasmines**, can provide good nest sites once they are established, but to my mind they are too fussy and need too much nurturing to be an asset to the bird garden.

One other climber that I like to grow purely because it often becomes infested with blackfly is the annual **nasturtium**. Remember how we all used to grow these at school and prided ourselves on the bright orange blossom? Now that I need a good supply of blackfly to feed small insectivorous birds, the ease of just putting seed into ordinary soil in April, where they are to grow, makes nasturtium an ideal plant for birds – either in hospital or just visiting the garden.

Small shrubs

Some birds prefer to nest low down beneath the reach of climbing plants. For these birds – marsh tits, willow warblers, yellow wagtails and sometimes robins – plant small shrubs purely for this purpose. *Cytisus kewensis*, a low **broom** with elegant arching stems, offers ideal shade and protection for smaller birds.

Mahonia japonica is an evergreen shrub that will grow in shade or in full sun. It also provides good cover for low-nesting birds and its pale yellow flowers bring a splash of colour in early February.

The epitome of a low shrub nesting site is the **gorse**, that brilliant yellow den of thorns that features on most of our heathland and commons. If you have the space, then plant a gorse or two; they may attract linnets, whitethroats, goldcrests, long-tailed tits, yellowhammers, bramblings and, if you live near moorland, a stonechat may even visit.

Window boxes and patios

Of course, some people do not have the luxury of a garden and have to rely on small window boxes or tubs set out on patios. A window box obviously cannot support the luxurious growth of a full-blown bird garden and is unlikely, normally, to attract nesting birds. There is, however, the wild mallard who, each year, lays and broods its egg in a window box high in the Barbican in London. You never can predict the whims of a nesting bird.

Basically, a window box should be at least 22.5 centimetres deep with the bottom 7.5 centimetres across filled with drainage such as broken flower pots and bricks or other rubble. It's not advisable to have drainage holes in the bottom of the box, as a constant trickle on people below would not be appreciated. Try to make the box very slightly wider than the sill or ledge it is to fit on and tilt it slightly backwards towards the window to prevent top soil running off during a rainstorm.

Basic garden soil will not contain enough nutrients to maintain much in the way of plant growth, so for every two parts of garden soil add one part leaf mould and one part coarse sand. Then, to every 1 metre of window box add two or three handfuls of bonemeal and one handful of general organic fertiliser. Moisten this mixture so that it just about binds together and fill the box to within 4 centimetres of the top. Then plant your plants and water them in.

The birdbath – even an old oven tray will be relished by the garden bird

We can't offer birds a great deal from a window box but some of the seed-bearing annuals will attract various colourful species. For instance, bullfinches go for the seeds of **pansies, wallflowers, antirrhinums** and **forget-me-nots**, often being joined by a pair of chaffinches. **Aster, poppy** and **Michael-mas daisy** seeds may attract goldfinches as well as the inevitable sparrows, tits and greenfinches.

The soil in your window box will need dampening every day and will be exhausted in 12–18 months. Then you can transplant any perennials, collect any leftover seeds from the annuals and start all over again.

The patio is quite different and will have the space and height available for much larger plants, grown in tubs which, like the window boxes, need watering every day. Species such as **honeysuckle** and **Russian vine** can be grown over trellis to encourage nesting black-birds and thrushes; berry-bearing plants like **cotoneaster** and **pyracantha** (great for a shaded patio) will give sustenance to winter visitors, even the very trusting waxwing.

All these plants will need watering until they are established, but to an extent this is true of those planted in a garden. Similarly both patio and garden should have a water feature, where birds can also find a drink or a bath, both in summer and winter.

Birdbaths, pools and ponds

Artificial birdbaths are fine, but are severely restricted in size and sometimes not much to look at. The complete answer to suit any patio or garden is to provide a pool of a size suited to the space available. Other than when it is frozen, the pool provides constant fresh water and, if shallow enough, gives the birds a place to bathe. Bird feathers are superbly engineered not just to provide a warm cover but also to be water-repellent. Most birds do not suffer from the cold, provided they have enough to eat. However, if a bird gets wet through it will soon chill and succumb. Feathers do not keep a bird dry because they are coated in preen oil, as some people would have it, but because they consist of interlocking barbs that, when the feathers overlap, form a perfect, waterproof raincoat. True, when birds are preening they do extract preen oil from a preen gland just above their tails. However, I regard this merely as a conditioner, making it easier for the feather mantle to slide into place. Most birds bathe every day, more so in the depths of winter when feather condition is of the utmost importance, so you may have to resort to an unfrozen birdbath to fulfil their requirements.

A good, well-balanced pool will provide everything a bird needs, with very little maintenance necessary to keep it clear. Once upon a time the task of building a pool meant 'puddling' a clay liner into the hole or else lining it with concrete and waiting weeks for it to cure (and then probably crack at the first severe frost). Nowadays there are all sorts of artificial liners, ranging from pre-formed fibre-glass ponds to sheets of heavy duty butyl, that are infinitely better and more reliable than their polythene equivalents. If you already have a fibre-glass or other prefabricated pool, it's a good idea to sink a heavy branch partially into it with one end overlapping the edge, making an escape route for any animal (or bird) that might fall in. Hedgehogs, for instance, are tremendous swimmers but are unable to climb the steep sides of some pools.

The first move in providing a garden pool is to decide on a site and peg the ground out to a required size and shape. Butyl should be black and comes in all sizes, so make your pool as large as you can, preferably with one edge facing an open or lawned area. Never site a pool beneath deciduous trees as the autumn leaf fall will decompose in the pond, using up valuable oxygen. If falling leaves are unavoidable, either scoop them out regularly or, in the autumn, cover the pond with netting, making sure its edges are well pegged down to prevent, once again, hedgehogs getting into trouble. Check a netting cover regularly in case grass snakes become entangled trying to reach the water.

Some of the pool should receive direct sunlight, to encourage plants to grow, but there should also be a calm, dappled area where amphibians can collect. Be careful though, for a small pond in direct sunlight could get too warm and boil the inhabitants.

After pegging out, mark out an area at the

Birdbaths – Ten Do's and Don't's

1 Don't use glycerine or any anti-freeze
2 Don't have water any deeper than 5 centimetres
3 Don't use smooth slippery containers, i.e. plastic bowls
4 Don't site a bath where cats can leap on to unwary birds
5 Don't forget to keep topping up water on below-zero days
6 Do put in gravel or rocks as safe-footing
7 Do put a nightlight underneath to keep the water ice-free
8 Do have qualified electrician fit any electric water heater
9 Do make a dust bath for sparrows and wrens
10 Do change the water regularly

---

lowest point where you can dig a soakaway for any water that overflows from the pond. This can be dug before starting on the pond and used as a place to dump all those bricks, rocks and other rubbish that turn up whenever you dig the garden. Mark your pegged site into three sections: the open side on to the lawn will be the beach, which should be dug to slope *gradually* from ground level down to about 10 centimetres below the pond surface. The opposite edge, next to the soakaway, should be a level, shallow area with a rim between it and the centre of the pond. This

will be marsh or bog area where marsh plants can be grown and birds can forage safely among the shallow weeds. The bog area will be soaked by overflow but care must also be taken that it does not dry out.

The central section of the pond too should slope *gradually* from the edge to a depth of 1 metre. This depth allows inhabitants to escape below if the pond freezes. When digging, remove any soil from the edges of the pool, where it will get in the way, and continue to do so through further stages of construction. (Do take precautions, like building a low wall around *any* pond, if young children are likely to be in the garden.)

Once the hole, shape, bog and beach areas are complete, remove any stones or sharp objects. Then either sieve your spoil soil all over the site, excluding the beach, to line it, or else use sand or damp newspaper. Next, offer up the butyl sheet, allowing a large overlap around the edge, which should be weighted down with large stones. As the water is added, its weight will stretch the butyl to fit the contours of the pond whilst the stones will hold the edges firm.

When the pond is full, trim and hide the edges under stones or turves. They need covering or the butyl may suffer from the sun's ultra-violet light. The bog area should be filled with soil and planted with bog plants

The heron can be an unwelcome garden bird because it is very fond of goldfish

such as *Veronica beccabunga* brooklime, *Myosotis palustris* water forget-me-not, or *Menyanthes trifoliata* bogbean – all of which are indigenous. I don't think that we are trying to benefit birds with water plants but the profusion of insects around any pond will attract the normal garden insectivores, together with the lightning raids of swifts, swallows and martins.

The last two species will also be grateful for the regular supply of mud for nestbuilding that a bog garden will offer.

The beach area should be filled as a gentle slope with 1 cm shingle interspersed with an occasional flat stone or rock. Birds are very wary when bathing and do like a good, all-round view. With the beach sloping up to the lawn, many more birds will 'take the plunge'.

The central, deep water area should be planted with suitable plants in special baskets. Birds will not take much notice of this area other than to hawk any insects that hatch out – midges and mosquitoes, for instance. A branch sticking out at a perpendicular angle will, however, provide a drinking perch for small birds such as wrens and warblers. I never recommend goldfish as pond inhabitants because they eat anything that breeds under the water, including tadpoles and smaller fish. Why not just get one or two jam jars full of sludge from a local pond and watch the wildlife in it soon make your new pool into a completely balanced community?

Should you come across a bird that looks as if it has drowned, don't give up immediately.

Instead, hold it upside down to drain any water from its trachea and then put it into a *very warm* place (see Chapter 10). Many birds will make a remarkable recovery once they are warmed up and dried. In fact, many apparently drowned birds have been saved by people miles from anywhere by the finder tucking the bird under their jumper or shirt. It's always worth a try.

The added attraction of water to a garden is that it sometimes acts as a magnet which attracts yellow and pied wagtails, marsh tits, pied flycatchers, reed buntings and sedge warblers to nest.

We have now been through a maze of natural ways to encourage birds into the garden to feed, bathe and nest. Sometimes the garden is not large enough to provide the planting space demanded by some species. In instances such as these, and in dire circumstances – for instance, when there is a prolonged spell of frozen weather – it is time to resort to artificial feeding stations, pools and food. It's usually in the second week of a cold spell that small birds start to succumb. So if extra provisions are made available during all frozen weather, there is more of a chance that many of the birds will survive.

5 They Can't Live on Bread Alone

The year is 1825. George the IV is on the throne of England, the future Queen Victoria is only six years old and there are no cars or network of railways. For most of the population it's a struggle to survive, and any wild bird, it's chick or eggs is a welcome addition to the dinner table. However, one man thought differently – John Freeman Dovaston. He valued the company of live wild birds and would not allow any on his estate to be harmed. He even went one step further in improving his relationship with the birds and erected probably the first ever bird table. Not, as we would recognise, a conventional bird table; Dovaston's 'ornithotrope' was a contraption consisting of a wooden hopper, iron hooks and harpsichord wire, all designed to move the feeding birds ever nearer to his window in order that he might observe much closer. He even started the bird tabler's twitching record, with twenty-three species seen on one winter's day.

The following year, 1826, Dovaston's great friend, the renowned wood engraver Thomas Bewick, published details of the ornithotrope in his *History of British Birds*. It sowed the seed of interest which was eventually to lead to the numerous British bird gardens of today being set up.

Mind you, although we British did finally get around to feeding wild birds, the practice took a long time to gather momentum. It may have been the well-known Victorian 'waste-not' attitude of society, along with the begging and poverty that were commonplace, which drastically slowed its progress.

Through the 1920s and thirties, however, the Western world gradually recovered from war and depression and it was the Americans who rejuvenated the practice of setting up bird tables. After the 1939–45 War, Britain followed suit, although I can only assume that, due to rationing, bird-table offerings were lacking in quality.

During the War, nobody in Britain had enough time to think of feeding wild birds; it was a hard enough job just staying alive. When, eventually, in 1946, peanuts were put

A cold, misty, winter morning, when blue tits and other small birds need all the food they can get

out for birds, it took them some time to get used to the easy meal and only when one bird was bold enough to feed did others slowly start to copy. Even the species that came to gardens were restricted, with birds such as great spotted woodpeckers never venturing near a peanut holder. There weren't even any collared doves – their invasion of this country did not start until one pair nested in 1955. But the more familiar garden birds – the tits, thrushes, finches, starlings and sparrows – soon relearnt the techniques of feeding from peanut holders and an assortment of weird and wonderful bird tables. They came to look on humans as essential providers of winter nourishment, so establishing the first rule of bird-tabling: '*Don't interrupt the regular daily supplies.*'

In winter, small birds such as robins need to consume about thirty per cent of their bodyweight every day, just to survive. And although we think of our feathered friends as 'bird-brains' they do, in fact, have a feeding strategy. Imagine if you were a robin who had regularly found food every day on a particular bird table. During a winter's day you can spend most of the daylight hours foraging elsewhere, knowing that on your way to roost there is the regular table with enough top-up nourishment to get you through the long, cold night ahead. Then, when you arrive, you find the table has not been replenished. It's too late to find more food. You are tired from searching all day for food and you know, deep down, that you are not going to survive the night. You fly to roost, tuck your head under your wing, lift one foot into your breast feathers to keep it warm and resign yourself to the fact that the empty bird table will cause you to perish.

It's as easy as that. In winter, even one slight hiccup in the supply of food can cause the deaths of not just one, but many birds. Happily, most bird tablers are diligent in keeping supplies topped up. It was estimated that in the severe winter of 1963, bird tables saved the lives of over one million small birds and, every year, bird tables alone are responsible for keeping the Swedish population of great tits to a viable number.

On snowy days even reed buntings will visit the garden looking for sustenance

If you think that these figures are astonishing, just imagine how many birds could be helped if we simply doubled the number of bird tables in existence. There are over fourteen million householders in Britain alone. Ten per cent of these buy food and nuts with the other forty per cent putting out bread and table scraps. It all helps, but *only if the bread is soaked first*. This not only prevents dry bread swelling in birds' crops but also stops marauding jackdaws flying off with whole slices of bread. If some of that forty per cent modified their offerings to include a few peanuts, then the added protein would mean more birds secure for the winter.

Bird-table Food – Ten Foods to Avoid

1 Any food containing salt
2 Desiccated coconut
3 Mouldy or damp peanuts
4 Currants (raisins and sultanas are fine)
5 Uncleaned maggots
6 Mealworms or maggots during the breeding season
7 Dry bread (can be used if soaked beforehand)
8 Any sticky foods
9 Citrus fruit
10 Raw vegetables

Peanuts

It may sound as if peanuts are the quick, easy answer to feeding birds, but in recent years their worth has caused complacency, with many birds dying from aflatoxin poisoning. Aflatoxin is a poison produced by a fungus which can develop on peanuts if they are not dried properly or are stored in humid conditions. The first problem-peanuts are, of course, peanuts which *were* perfectly all right but which were then stored in a damp shed or cellar. It is our responsibility to make sure that we only supply fresh, dry peanuts bought from a reputable dealer. This brings us to the other source of aflatoxins – cheap peanuts bought in from South America. There are laws about the level of aflatoxins in food for humans and domestic animals but, as usual, wildlife is ignored, allowing the chronic poison (250 parts per billion can *kill* a horse) to be bought openly on loose peanuts. Thankfully, the strong bird lobby in this country has got together and formed the Birdfood Standards Association to monitor these sorts of problems. Now, imported peanuts are inspected and, if sound, the importer is allowed to display the B.S.A. Seal of Approval. Look for it, it means: 'We're safe nuts.'

The other bird killer that can be found on peanuts is salt. Most birds, other than sea birds, cannot cope with salt of any kind, so salted peanuts are out, as are crisps and all salted food.

Fruit & mixed bird food

America, even though it is a peanut-producing nation, surprisingly uses very few peanuts on its bird tables. And, although Americans spend £68 million a year on wild-bird food, the food they offer consists predominantly of **suet**, **mixed bird seed**, **fruit**, **maize** and **sunflower seed**. These all feature in British bird-table fare and can be used by that forty per cent, although I must stress that fruit does not mean citrus fruit or currants, which are indigestible to birds. **Apples** and **pears** cut in half and put out 'sunny side up' are great favourites with all the thrushes and serve as life-savers at two critical times of the year.

The first is the summer, when there is a prolonged period of drought, with worms and other ground invertebrates burying deep into

A cock blackbird, who will appreciate a few sliced apples at any time of the year

the baked soil, leaving blackbirds, in particular, without their main source of moisture. A few sliced apples a day will save the lives of your local pack of blackbirds and even their juvenile fledglings if they haven't flown the nest. Song thrushes are luckier. They have learnt the technique of breaking snails' shells on their 'anvils', giving them a continuously available source of sustenance and moisture. For some reason, blackbirds have never learned the technique, although they will readily pirate the opened snail once the thrush has done all the demolition work.

The second time when fruit can be a life-saver is at the opposite end of the year, when there has been a prolonged cold spell. Then the redwings, fieldfares, mistle and other migratory thrushes soon start to suffer hunger pangs and move into orchards and gardens, joining the local blackbirds and thrushes in a desperate search for windfall apples and pears. Then is the time to scatter apples at the far end of the garden. These Scandinavian thrushes will not venture nearer than that, but that fruit could be their lifeline. If you have fruit trees it's always worth storing apples and pears in trays ready for the winter. Remember, though, that one bad apple can infect the rest. Put it out on the bird table – it will be eaten no matter what condition it's in and it may have a nice juicy grub at the centre as a bonus.

Worms & slugs

Of course, you can help blackbirds and other worm feeders in the height of summer by laying a compost of mulch over all exposed soil. This will keep the topsoil moist and encourage worms and other invertebrates to stay near the surface. Turning some of the mulch over each morning will encourage blackbirds and robins to forage amongst the leaves. Laying a sheet of black polythene on the lawn overnight will also expose some worms when you take it off again and it will attract slugs – although these will only be taken as a last resort.

It's also worthwhile turning compost heaps in cold or dry weather to expose invertebrates, but do be careful that there isn't a hibernating or resting hedgehog in it, or, for that matter, any other animal which may be availing itself of your heap's hospitality.

Insects & grubs

Although it will make many people cringe, live food is the essence of life for most wild birds. In fact, apart from the columbids – the pigeons and doves – and, possibly, sparrows, all other garden birds feed their young on insects and grubs. We can help out by providing live food but, unfortunately, the types which are easily available – **mealworms** and clean fishing **maggots** – are too tough-skinned to be offered to baby birds. For this reason, they should not be put out during the breeding months, which are March to September. There is, however, a new type of live food on the market which we are going to try this year with our orphaned birds. Called 'Waxworm. The *Safe* Soft Option' it is a high-energy food with soft thin skins, easily digested, even by young birds. The 'worms' can be stored for several weeks at 12–15°C but, as I see it, their drawback is cost – about £3.22 per hundred. For this reason I would not recommend putting a bowl of them in front of a flock of starlings because your £3.22 will disappear in an instant. However, if you know of a one-parent family where the surviving bird is struggling to rear a family on its own, then offer it Waxworm on the quiet, away from all the other 'gannets'.

Mealworms, or more correctly, the larvae of the beetle *Tenebrio molitor*, are the other highly priced but valuable live food used by many aviculturists to feed their prize birds. Their benefits far outweigh their drawbacks – that too many can cause a condition akin to gout and that stray larvae will actually chew into nestlings. On their plus side, they are full of protein, can be bred and grown at home and, more importantly, are a certain way to a robin's heart.

Any robin will sell its soul for a mealworm and most can be gradually encouraged to come to the hand for their favourite titbit. To start with, throw a few crumbs of cake on to the ground, where a robin will come down to feed. Once it has settled to that, include a mealworm or two. Once tasted never forgotten, so continue for a couple of days with the occasional mealworm and then put down a small dish or lid with two or three mealworms in it, all the time moving slowly nearer and nearer to the feeding site. Crouching down and not staring directly at the bird will make it feel more at ease.

When you are within touching distance of the food, and the robin still comes, place the back of your hand on the ground, keeping the bowl, with its one or two mealworms, on your upturned palm. If the robin still feeds, then, over a period of days, gradually offer the bowl at an increased height until finally you are standing up. After a few more days the bowl can be left out altogether and the robin will come direct to your hand and will soon fly to you whenever you offer up a mealworm. Just two points to remember: always reward the robin's visit with a mealworm and never make any sudden, unexpected movements.

As I have said, mealworms can be very expensive, but the cost can be considerably reduced by 'growing' them at home to ensure a continuous supply. They should be cultivated in a wooden box about the size of a biscuit tin, with small holes drilled in the top to allow ventilation. Sometimes tin boxes are recommended, but I have always found that wood is superior in that it allows the culture to drain properly. On the bottom of the box, lay a piece of hessian or sacking. On this should be scattered some bran and slices of potato, covered with pieces of bread. Then lay another piece of hessian on top, with the bran potato and bread added as before. A third layer of hessian, bran potato and bread is all that is needed to complete the arrangement. About one hundred mealworms can be added and will immediately crawl in between the layers and begin feeding on the bran and potato. As the mealworms grow they will regularly shed their skin until they are mature enough to pupate. After this they will change into small black beetles, which will in turn lay eggs in the stale pieces of bread. These will hatch and the cycle will start all over again. Potato should be added at intervals to supply fresh food and moisture. As the larger mealworms can be cannibalistic, it's a good idea to have several cultures on the go, each at different stages of development.

There are also other live foods that you can culture yourself. I wouldn't recommend growing maggots as these metamorphose into bluebottles and blowflies – hardly desirable – but by all means purchase white, clean **maggots** from an angling shop. They are comparatively cheap and are easily obtained throughout the winter. They can be stored in a refrigerator for a few weeks, but should be used up as soon as they start to pupate. Small birds such as tits or wrens may prefer the smaller maggots known to anglers as pinkies or squats. Just make sure they are undyed and are cleaned.

Far less gruesome to keep and easy to culture are **brandlings**, *Eisenia foetida*, small earthworms which flourish on compost or discarded kitchen waste. As described by Jack Temple for the Soil Association, a good 'worm compost' will produce a population explosion of brandlings as well as regular loads of superior garden compost. Quite briefly, you need a dustbin with a close-fitting lid. Make about a dozen small holes in the lid for aeration and two rings of small holes for drainage, one about 7.5 centimetres and another at 15 centimetres from the bottom of the bin. Fill the bottom of the bin with about 15 centimetres of small stones and sand and then cover with two or three pieces of wood, leaving about 1.25 centimetres between them.

Then fill about one fifth of the remainder of the bin with *well-rotted* manure. (You can use peat but currently there is the problem that too much is being extracted from the low levels.) Put in about a hundred brandlings, purchased from an angling shop, or you can introduce your own shovelful of manure, which will have its own 'starter pack'.

Now to feed the brandlings. Add well-shredded vegetable waste or well-soaked newspaper, liberally mixed with calcified seaweed (available from gardening centres). The calcified seaweed will keep the compost alkaline, a state much preferred by brandlings. If the bin does become too acid, the brandlings will die and will be replaced by white worms, *Enchytraeids*, which will have the same effects but are far more difficult to collect for feeding to birds. (*Enchytraeids*, however, are much favoured by fish, especially the smaller species.)

Do not fill the dustbin in one go. In the beginning just add about 15 centimetres of shredded waste every three weeks or so. Sprinkle each layer with a little leaf-mould and some water if the compost looks dry. Any water draining from the bottom of the bin should be collected and used as organic liquid manure. Eventually the whole binful will become loose, friable Super Compost for use on the garden. But before using it all, take one shovelful, worms and all, to start your next culture.

Once a bin is underway, there is always a source of available worms to be put out, in a dish, on the bird table – welcome protein, especially in the depths of winter.

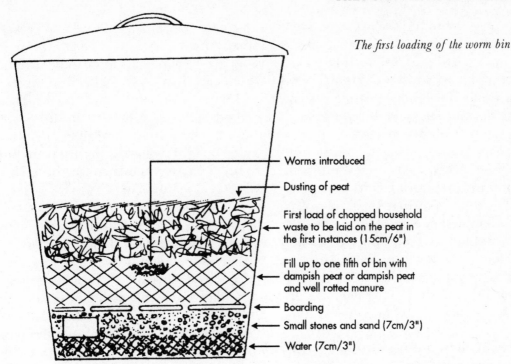

The first loading of the worm bin

Worms introduced

Dusting of peat

First load of chopped household waste to be laid on the peat in the first instances (15cm/6")

Fill up to one fifth of bin with dampish peat or dampish peat and well rotted manure

Boarding

Small stones and sand (7cm/3")

Water (7cm/3")

You have probably gathered that bird-table feeding is a winter occupation. In fact, apart from offering moist foods in a drought, it's not advisable to put food on the tables during the summer months of April to September. Most of the familiar garden birds will probably ignore your goodies as there will be plenty of protein-rich live food in the woods and hedgerows. Some birds may take your dried food titbits to their young, who will be quite incapable of digesting peanuts or bread. Throughout the summer just offer water for drinking and bathing and watch your garden birds come back for more.

Other foods

During the winter, any food is acceptable, but apart from the protein-rich peanuts and live food, there are other foods which will give just as much benefit to a tiny bird. **Suet**, for instance, is a great favourite, whether offered in small pieces or smeared on trees for tits, goldcrests, wrens, tree creepers and nuthatches. One novel idea is to get an old birch log and to drill a few holes into the soft wood. Fill the holes with suet and hang the log up – it makes a superb attraction for great spotted woodpeckers. I am not very domesticated, but I am assured that *short* suet is the stuff to use.

Suet is very warming, as are any **meat products**: the carcase of the Christmas turkey or any meat bones are readily picked clean, especially by starlings. **Hemp seed** provides a wonderful central heating system, although I am not sure about its addictive qualities. All forms of **mixed seed** are readily taken; to keep the cost down stay away from the glamorous, cage-bird mixes and use **mixed corn** instead, sprinkled once a week with a little vitamin powder.

One old chap we know lives just to be with 'his' birds, and he swears by **porridge oats**, especially for collared doves. Following his lead, I use them at the hospital to get some of the younger birds feeding. Porridge oats are also ideal for giving to orphaned wood mice and voles.

Sliced, **cooked potatoes**; **sultanas**; **raisins**; **dried fruitcake**; **boiled conkers** and, of course, **wild seeds** are just a few alternative feeds. The list can be endless so try a few of your own, bearing in mind the *no-no's* of soft and sticky. Common sense and the birds themselves will tell you if the food you put out is any good.

Bird tables

I have described various sorts of food, but haven't suggested any method of presenting them safely to the birds. Of course, what we need initially is a bird table – or bird feeding station, as they are now known. It can be just a simple tray or an elaborate affair with a roof to protect the bird-table fare and to keep off larger birds like crows, jackdaws and jays (who are very partial to peanuts), and all of whom can clear a bird table in minutes.

Making your own table is the cheapest method of providing a feeding station, although there are several good models which can be bought by mail order from a reputable source. I say reputable source because there are several features which are essential to the success of the feeding station and the safety of the birds, features which reputable manufacturers bear in mind. Most importantly, any bird table should measure at least 75×60 centimetres. This allows the food to be spread out and gives enough room for the free-for-all and sparring that will inevitably take place. It's often said that one bird, on finding food, will attract its mates. I have been close to many birds and, apart from a parent's, or sometimes even another adult's, benevolent attitude towards young birds, I have observed all birds to be very selfish. The last thing they want to do is share their find with others.

There should be a lip to the table top – a barrier of about 4 centimetres on all four sides – to prevent seed and crumbs from flying off the edges. Mind you, a certain amount of spillage will serve those species who probably won't venture on to the table top: the dunnocks, song thrushes and wood mice.

Nuthatches are spending more and more time in gardens, feeding on suet or peanuts

However hard you try to deter them, squirrels will find a way to reach your bird table

Bird Tables – Ten Do's and Don't's

1 Don't erect a bird table if you own a cat
2 Don't interrupt the regular daily supplies
3 Don't use rustic or rough poles to support the bird table
4 Don't site the bird table within six feet of a potential launching point of a leaping squirrel or cat
5 Don't use the roof of a bird table as a nest box
6 Do put out fresh food in the morning and again in the afternoon
7 Do make sure that there is always unfrozen drinking water available (never add glycerine or anti-freeze)
8 Do clean the bird table at least once a week with a 10 per cent ammonia solution
9 Do shelter the table in winter from north and east winds
10 Do slope the table slightly to assist drainage

There should be a gap in the barrier at each corner, both to facilitate drainage and to help with the cleaning, which should be carried out at least once a week using a ten per cent ammonia solution. To assist drainage further, the table should be set to slope slightly, altering the position regularly to protect any grass underneath.

There are two ways of mounting a bird table safely. It can be hung from a branch by wires to each corner. Selecting as slender a branch as possible will help deter cats but the master pirate, the squirrel, will still find its way to clear the table of goodies.

The alternative is to mount the table on an upright pole between 1.35 and 2 metres above the ground. Here is where your choice of table is crucial: completely ignore those picturesque rustic types on sale at many garden centres. These are an open invitation to cats and squirrels to climb up easily to the platform. Cats can be deterred by using a smooth wooden pole but even a plastic drainpipe will not deter the squirrel. For him, an upsidedown biscuit tin or cone of metal is the only solution.

Never, ever, have a nest box sited in the roof of the table, as the hassle between tenants and table visitors can be alarming. By all means, though, have a roof over the table. This not only gives some protection from the weather but will prevent the larger birds scoffing everything offered. And of course it prevents the local sparrowhawk or kestrel from snatching your guests from the table, that is if the guests have so little sense as to remain still.

A roof on the bird table also, unfortunately, makes a good launch pad for cats, squirrels and corvids. A covering of loose wire netting will prove very useful as a deterrent.

Cats and squirrels are the main menace to bird tables and, as they can both leap prodigious distances, any table should be situated at least 2 metres from any likely jumping-off point. In fact, most bird-table birds prefer a 2-metre open space on all sides of the table, although an occasional perch at that distance will encourage the wary to approach that much nearer, especially if the table is in the centre of a wide open space.

The pole of a table that is sunk into the ground should be held upright by sinking a few bricks around the base. There are, however, two disadvantages to a permanent site. Firstly, no matter how clean you keep the table and its surroundings, the ground beneath it will soon become soiled and sour. A movable table with a huge, cruciform foot on it can be positioned at a fresh site and can also be moved nearer to your observation point

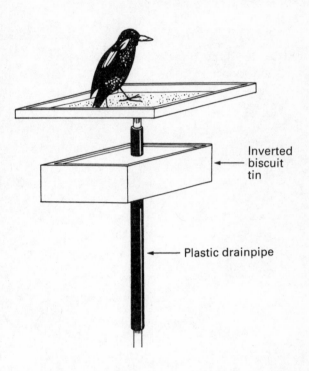

An effective method of preventing mammals from reaching a bird table

Inverted biscuit tin

Plastic drainpipe

once the birds get used to your presence, whereas a permanent table has to stay where it is, with you having to get nearer to it: action that is guaranteed to disturb even your regular bird visitors.

Birdbaths & drinking water

If you should want to photograph your garden birds it is absolutely essential that

they are near your vantage point. But better than a feeding station close by would be a birdbath or a source of drinking water. After all, most of those wonderful wildlife photographs from Africa are patiently obtained after hours sitting concealed by a water-hole – a situation we can emulate in our own back gardens.

Water is truly the fluid of life. Birds can starve to death in severe conditions, but without water they would perish in a quarter of the time. Whenever a good samaritan phones in to report having picked up an injured bird, we explain that it will more than likely survive not feeding for a day or two but just a few hours without water can cause irreparable damage. Mind you, I still will not recommend that a novice should try to give any bird a drink. More birds are drowned with pipettes or fountain pen fillers than by any other source. I know this sounds like a defeatist attitude, but we would rather the bird is brought to us or taken to an experienced rehabilitator than it should be killed by kindness. However, always offer a very shallow bowl of water to any bird that can stand, because it can probably drink for itself.

In the wild, most birds must drink and bathe regularly and would not survive long without water for both activities. Birds of prey, however, do not normally drink water,

The ideal bird table – safe and with a plentiful supply of food

but may well visit the garden for an early morning bath and easily caught breakfast. But don't panic, this is a very rare occurrence and should not deter planned water bath facilities that complete a bird garden.

A bird's feathers and their condition are the difference between life and death for them. Feathers are the bird's raincoat, which will leak if not in tip-top condition. Just one breakthrough can cause a fatal chilling, even at the height of summer and, of course, makes it inevitable in the depths of winter. At this time, too, the feathers act as an insular barrier against the energy-sapping cold. Feathers that are out of condition could allow the precious body heat to percolate out, resulting in the downward spiral of hypothermia.

The third vital function of feathers is their ability to enable a bird to fly, courtesy of their being so light, with intrinsic qualities of aerodynamics and strength. Badly conditioned feathers tend to bend, crack or even break, greatly impairing a bird's flying prowess in evading predators, feeding on the wing or, in the case of birds of prey, of actually hunting.

Every bird will spend considerable time each day cleaning and grooming each feather, many of them with the special preen-oil conditioner taken by the beak from the preen gland just above the tail. Any feather contamination would impair the efficacy of the preen oil, allowing those fatal cracks or fractures to develop. To make sure of pristine plumage, most birds must bathe in either water or dust, even in the coldest times of winter, when unfrozen water cannot be found. Bathing in dust helps to remove particles of grease and dirt from the feathers, rather like our cleaning greasy hands in sand.

This is where we come in, by providing bathing facilities as well as equally vital drinking water. We can make up for many of the natural watering places that have been filled in by farmers and developers.

Any old water container will do, from the dog's bowl to a resplendent statuesque cupid holding a basin above his head. None of them should be more than 5 centimetres deep, although a bed of gravel, preferably sloping, would provide shallow conditions in deeper utensils.

Some of the most frequented birdbaths are simply upturned metal dustbin lids raised on two or three bricks. Using metal instead of plastic gives the birds a much surer footing and when sited on a good lawn doesn't look too far out of place, even though it is only a dustbin lid.

Another advantage of the dustbin lid birdbath is that a slow-burning nightlight can be set underneath to keep the water from freezing during the short, winter days. One suggested method of keeping a birdbath free of ice recommends sinking it into a box of moulding hay. True, it will work, but anyone dealing with birds should avoid damp or moulding hay because it is a source of the dreadful fungus *Aspergillus*, which can be re-sponsible for the deaths of many captive birds.

There are now on the market several small electric heaters that can be immersed in the birdbath, as can various aquarium heaters. Particular care, however, should be taken with electricity in the garden, with birdbath heaters preferably being installed by qualified electricians.

Sometimes glycerine is mentioned as an anti-freeze but this can have disastrous effects in destroying a bird's plumage.

In general, birds seem to prefer the feeding station that has water on offer and I know how, in our bird wards every morning, the patients are queueing up for their baths, even before they start feeding. I have to be careful about the sizes of our birdbaths because a bird slightly impaired in its movements can lose its balance and easily drown. In the garden, with fully fit wild birds, it is quite safe to have all different sizes, as long as the depth is controlled. In fact, the dustbin lid, when not doubling as a birdbath, makes an ideal template to make a more aesthetic concrete bath which can be mounted on a variety of stands.

The baths can be made from sand and cement mixed in proportions of three to one. Most builders' merchants do now supply ready-mixed bags of concrete ideal for the D I Y enthusiast. Simply add water and mix thoroughly, then lay it around the interior of the dustbin lid to a thickness of about 2.5 centimetres. After a few days it will have set and can be carefully removed, ready for weathering. But don't let the birds use it yet. Instead, each day for ten days, soak it in fresh water to flush out any chemical residues in the concrete.

After this the bath can be mounted on various simple-to-erect stands. One possibility is to mount the bath on four pieces of 7.5 centimetre square timber held in position with four lengths of 2.5 centimetre timber. Cutting the tops of the four legs at an angle to match the slope of the bottom of the bath makes for a more stable structure.

The other method is even more labour-saving, with the bath stood simply on the top of an upright length of earthenware drainage pipe. Both look quite pleasing, especially if coloured concrete is used for the tops.

The three-in-one cement mix can prove very useful for moulding all manner of baths. A typical example is where an old tree stump is left for the benefit of insects and birds. If a tray-like wooden frame is made to enclose the top, then concrete can be poured in and fashioned like a birdbath, preferably with a sloping, rough bottom. After three days the timber frame can be removed, then with the ten-day weathering treatment complete, the bath will sit safely on the roughest surface.

All birdbaths should be to roughly the same depth of 5 centimetres. And *roughly* is the word, as the rougher the surface, the safer it is for the birds.

The sparrows and pigeons will decline to use the birdbath, but may well shower in the spray created by other birds. Nothing is more comical than to see a pigeon lift one wing so that the spray can penetrate under its 'arm' – a practice very often observed during light summer showers. Sparrows and pigeons, together with the wrens, prefer dust baths. We can also provide these in the garden by arranging shallow pits of finely sieved sand and ashes in unwatered parts of the garden. Also, an occasional dusting of pyrethrum to the dust bath will help counteract feather lice and other ectoparasites.

Just as with bird tables, the siting of birdbaths can be crucial for the safety of your avian visitors. If they don't feel safe then they won't come. Make sure any birdbath is out in the open, as birds realise that they are at their most vulnerable when up to their eyes in bathing and insist on a good all-round view of their surroundings.

If you are not D I Y-minded and would prefer to buy a ready-made birdbath in garden centres, there are always several ornate varieties, some of which are practical while others are obviously useless. As I say, watch the depth of water and avoid anything made of marble. Marble, especially if it's holding water, is very likely to crack under freezing conditions.

The latest type of birdbath available is pre-cast from fibreglass and seems to fulfil all the requirements for a garden bird's *toilette*.

6 Nest-building

Almost unnoticed in the hectic world of the garden or woodland edge, a small branch snaps from a maturing tree and leaves a small scar, ignored by everything except tiny, invisible fungus spores floating on the wind, searching for somewhere to spread their decay. Silently, they settle, easing their all-consuming tendrils into the still-healthy wood. Slowly, over the next couple of years, their march spreads the softness of their passing into the main body of the tree.

Their progress goes on, still unnoticed until, on a fine March day, a freshly coupled pair of willow tits, out house-hunting, spot the decay and home in on the tree's weakness. They chip away at the softened wood together until a cavity is formed which is large enough to house their expected brood of up to nine young willow tits. For the next five weeks the hole is full of life and comings and goings as the family grows, until that bright early morning when they are gone, leaving the hole empty but far from dead.

The hole's initial creators, the fungi, are still thriving and gnawing away at the wholesome wood. As they do so, the hole grows until, by next spring, it is too large to suit the tiny willow tits but proves ideal for their larger cousins, the great tits.

Another family thrives in the hole, soon leaving it to grow even larger, suitable for the next year's avian tenants.

But the following March, nobody wants to know the larger hole. It sits, cold and empty until, in the middle of April, a small black-and-white bird peers into the cave, quickly signals its mate, and a pair of pied flycatchers (those summer visitors to the north and west of England) take up residence. They will, in future, always come back to the same nest site. But when they return the following year, they are too late – fellow migrants who arrive slightly earlier, the redstarts, have taken over the hole.

Disappointed but not dismayed, the pied flycatchers move to a vacant nest box that a thoughtful gardener had kept blocked until their late arrival.

After the redstarts have raised their brood, the family fly off, this time to Africa. The hole sits, silently growing, half-expecting that most peculiar bird, the wryneck, to move in before the redstarts return the following April. But there are no wrynecks left breeding in this country so, instead, a pair of glorious, great spotted woodpeckers chisel the hole to suit themselves, only to be ousted by a pair of bustling starlings. Thankfully, the gardener spots the eviction and tries the old trick of putting a golf ball into the nest hole. Most hole-nesting birds have white or whitish eggs, but for some reason starlings will not nest around a golf ball. Great spotted woodpeckers will, on the other hand, or so it is said.

However, the woodpeckers, having been disturbed, choose to nest elsewhere and a pair of nuthatches sidle down the tree to take over the hole. As always, the hole is not to the liking of Mrs Nuthatch, who promptly plasters the entrance with mud until only she and her spouse can find the way in.

So successful is the nest site that the nuthatches manage to raise two broods, but the effort of housing the two families has been to the detriment of the hole, with the fungus relentlessly working its way further and further into the tree. To add to this, rainwater begins to find a channel in the tree bark that leads directly into the hole and it now becomes a very efficient reservoir. The gardener spots the flooding too late and although he bores two drainage holes, the damage done is irreparable, for the hole has grown too large for any of its previous tenants.

The gardener realises this and forgets about the empty hole until, two years later, minute squeaks cause him to climb up and peer into the blackness. Two ugly little chicks covered in blue down squeak up at him, wobbling their grotesque beaks in his direction. They seem dry, so his drainage hole must be working, but what species of bird are they, he wonders. A harsh cooing to his right soon tells him that these are stock doves, the often misrepresented countryside member of the *Columbidae*, the pigeons and doves.

He scuttles down his ladder and watches from a distance as the two devoted parents visit and revisit the hole. He can only imagine the two 'squeakers' stretching up to feed on the rich 'pigeon's milk' which is secreted from the lining of the adults' throats.

When feeding orphaned baby columbids, it is necessary to try to re-create the parent's feeding behaviour by offering a liquified feed which the 'squeakers' can suck up. Only pigeons and doves can draw fluids up in this manner; to drink, other birds have to take a mouthful of water and then lift their heads to swallow.

The size of the hole would also have suited a pair of kestrels, and I particularly remember an incident when two orphan stock doves were brought into the hospital because their 'mother' had been found lying dead with them in the nest hole. The dead bird was a

A blue tit in a man-made nest box

The next tenants' babies, however, are the complete opposite – wonderful, almost-cuddly tawny owl chicks, bobbing and head-swaying at the gardener as he peers into the cavity, which is now enormous. He always makes sure that the parents aren't at home because tawny owls, like other birds of prey, can be very aggressive in defence of their nests.

Over the next three weeks the male tawny owl brings food for the female to tear for the chicks. And then they are swallowing their food whole, so both parents are needed to hunt to keep their two youngsters fed. When they are five weeks old, though, they can fly away with their parents to practise the hunting skills that, although inherent, still need sharpening up in the field, so to speak.

They leave behind them a very old hole that, still growing, has become too large to be of use to any nesting bird. Now the gardener moves in to refashion the hole to suit some of the smaller species which had nested in it before it grew out of all proportion.

He shapes an old piece of wood to fit into the hole and then cuts a 5 centimetre square hole at the top before holding it in place with a length of wood extending beyond the edges and screwed to the tree. Covering the screws with Vaseline before fixing makes them easier to remove at the end of the season, in order to clean out any old nest material and un-hatched eggs that can be a source of infection if left to rot.

kestrel, obviously having succumbed during a previous tenancy. Needless to say, we immediately had the two baby stock doves put back into their nest, where their parents continued to rear them.

Now back to our hole – the stock doves have flown by the end of April, after which a pair of jackdaws, evicted from a nearby chimney stack, move in and raise their ungainly babies. All orphan jackdaws that end up with us are known as 'Terry Dactyl' because of their undeniable likeness to those prehistoric flying monsters.

The great spotted woodpeckers at last move back into their hole, which can now be tailored each year to suit their requirements.

This hole lives on and only because the gardener has intervened to stem the process of decay. Normally we should not interfere with the natural process but, in my opinion, the dearth of decent nest trees has been caused by man and we should try to recompense wild birds by providing suitable nest sites.

Existing nest sites

The provision of various nest boxes is the obvious way of encouraging birds to nest, but nothing is guaranteed and as birds are notoriously fickle, it's worth trying out existing possibilities before indulging in purpose-made nest boxes.

Take a look around the garden. Try to imagine potential nest sites. Of course, you are unlikely to enthuse about the suitability of an unmade bed, as one pair of robins did, or on the comfort to be found inside a skull hanging on a gibbet. Blackbirds are notorious for nesting on mechanical objects such as car wheels or tractor engines, bringing transport to a standstill while the family is raised. Mind you, sometimes the transport isn't grounded and I am reminded of the house martins who nested on a Scandinavian ferry successfully and fed their mobile youngsters on a floating course between ports.

Sometimes these unusual nests can cause serious problems and then they have to be moved. Providing there is no alternative, a nest can be moved, but only a very short distance and then only with the utmost care. For two days before the move, mark the nest with brightly coloured ribbon or paper. Then, in full view of the nesting birds, place the nest smoothly and quietly in a more convenient position close by its original setting. Then stand well back and make sure the adults return. It's the sound of the young nestlings calling that persuades the parents to recommence feeding. The brightly coloured ribbon acts as a stimulating marker of the nest, while the calling of the youngsters encourages the parents into forgetting that the nest has been moved.

Drastic action such as moving a nest should only be taken as a last resort and definitely never with a robin's nest, as the birds will more than likely desert, leaving you with cold eggs or starving youngsters. In fact, although nest boxes can be inspected for contents, the possibility of desertion by the adults makes the practice fraught with danger. I much prefer to watch the comings and goings of, first one bird (the male as he feeds the brooding female), and then both birds as they feed the youngsters, who can be heard clamouring for food at each visit. If you do open or look into a nest containing nearly fully fledged youngsters, they are likely to 'explode' out of the nest. Picking them up and simply putting them back in the nest will only result in another explosion. The safest method is to collect them all together, put them in the nest and cover them or the nest hole with a piece of cloth for at least ten minutes. Then slowly remove the cloth and, hopefully, the youngsters will stay put.

There are laws about approaching nest sites which, coupled with the dangers of explosion and desertion, make the practice of checking nest contents one to be avoided.

But you can watch from a distance, especially if you plan to position your potential nest sites near to your living room – your birdwatcher's hide with all the comforts of home. Different species have their own preferences for nesting places; the most popular with garden birds, though, is the 'hole nest'. Suitable holes are easy to create, but just as important are the simple ledges and trays to suit the blackbirds, thrushes, robins and those great little aerialists, the spotted flycatchers.

The eaves: swallows, house martins & swifts

Swallows, house martins and swifts will always return to their previous year's nest, so it's important that these are not disturbed. During the winter you will be able to set up camouflaged observation points to allow you to watch the parent birds' comings and goings to their youngsters during the breeding season. However, the house martins and swift's preference for nesting in high eaves may test your innovative skills.

House martins will always build their mud nests in the right angle between a wall and an overhanging eave. Swifts will actually nest in holes in the eave, preferring to fly in from below. I know of one roof where nest boxes, with viewing panels, have been fitted over the holes in the eaves so that the growth of the swiftlets can be monitored. This arrangement has also proved to be ideal for us to introduce orphaned swiftlets to a foster family.

Swallows, unlike these other summer visitors, seem to prefer to nest in dark, dingy outbuildings, often gaining access via a broken window or a gap in the door frame. To encourage their return the following spring, these entrances should be left unimpeded or they may well move elsewhere.

Their mud nests are usually built on beams or ledges and may be used time and time again, although they will not be used for consecutive broods – presumably to break the life cycle of any parasites breeding in the old nest material.

Since swallows, house martins and swifts naturally return to their previous nest, they make ideal subjects for the armchair birdwatcher who does not want to get involved in making nest boxes or creating artificial nest sites.

Brick or stone walls

If your eaves have failed to attract these choosy visitors and if your garden does not contain mature trees and shrubs, don't de-

House martins nesting

spair. Many of the best nest sites can be fashioned from brick or stone walls, and they may even attract a pair of strutting pied wagtails, who won't take a second look at a conventional nest box. Simply remove a single brick from any wall (or, better still, leave a brick out during construction) and you have a cavity sufficient for the nest of not only wagtails but wrens, robins and spotted flycatchers or 'wall birds' as they are known in Buckinghamshire.

A standard brick is 22.5 centimetres wide, 7.6 centimetres high and 10 centimetres deep and, by fixing a length of wood along the front edge of the cavity, you will form a sheltered ledge site.

Pied wagtails may also be attracted if the hole is partially closed using a slice of brick which is cemented in, leaving a gap of 4 centimetres at one end. The little cave formed may also be found and used by some members of

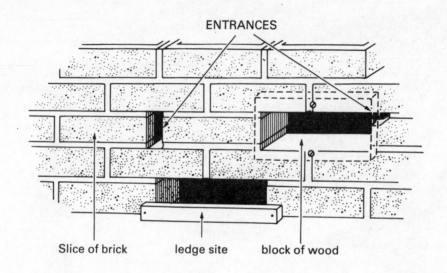

ENTRANCES

Slice of brick   ledge site   block of wood

Three types of nest site that can be created by removing single bricks from a wall

the tit family. At the end of each season, the slice of brick will need to be knocked out in order to clean out the contents.

A variation of the old 'brick out of the wall' trick is to cover the hole completely with a piece of timber. The entrance hole to the cavity is then chipped from the corner of an adjoining brick. Once again, this site can prove desirable to pied wagtails or blue tits.

The drawing shows the three types of 'brick out of the wall' nest sites described, in close proximity to one another. This would undoubtedly lead to confrontation and ideally the sites should be positioned at least 1.2 metres apart.

Of course, leaving bricks out during construction saves a lot of chipping away at solid mortar, but a better idea originates from Germany, where you can get brick-size cement nest boxes specifically designed to be included in new constructions. Although they are intended for high-flying swifts, they can be included lower down a wall, where they would prove to be eminently suitable for other species such as blue tits and flycatchers.

Those gardeners fortunate enough to have traditional, dry stone walls around the garden, will be able to create all sorts of nooks and crannies simply by moving a few stones around. The naturally formed tunnels between the stones are great favourites with blue tits, wrens and wood mice, while in some more remote coastal areas they could even be inhabited by petrels.

Tree nest sites

Happily, though, most gardens have a tree of some sort that can lend itself perfectly to the improvisation of nest sites. Most larger species of tree do not possess sites that would attract birds to nest. There are, of course, exceptions – notably the old, gnarled pollarded willows, with their many mysterious cavities, and even very ancient apple trees, where holes are beginning to develop. However, our garden trees are seldom old enough or are too well cared for to have cavities and it's these that can be dressed to provide the potential nest sites that would otherwise be missing.

Firstly, strips of sacking can be fixed beneath branches and stubs to form hammocks. Fixing the sacking firmly, with strips of wood nailed to the tree, makes it easily replaceable when it eventually rots. Hammocks have proved to be very popular with wrens, in particular: they seem to appreciate the dark shady caverns produced by the sacking.

Sacking hammocks can, in fact, be slung in any out-of-the-way place: in an open shed, under the eaves, or tucked up in the corner of a pergola or arbour.

Earlier on in this chapter I described the life of a hole created by willow tits. Your

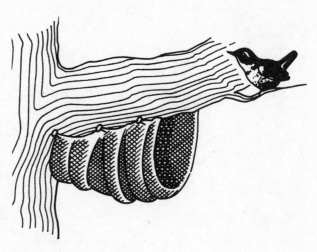

Hammocks fashioned from sacking are suitable for wrens

garden trees, however, may already have small holes or depressions that are quite unsuitable as nest sites. Many can be tailored to the liking of spotted flycatchers and robins by tacking a piece of wood, or bark, across the lower front of the hole, allowing a brooding bird unhindered vision over the front. These small sites are extremely popular with willow tits and, in Scotland, the crested tits.

Very shallow depressions in the side of a tree trunk or branch can similarly be adapted to form nest sites for other small birds, especially tree creepers. Quite simply, nail a piece of bark over the depression, leaving just a small gap for the bird to enter and even wrens may take up your offer. Also, pieces of bark simply nailed to the trunk of a tree, leaving a small space behind, have proved

very popular, once again, with tree creepers for both roosting and nesting. In fact, if any small depression in the trunk of a tree, especially the giant Wellingtonia, is found decorated with white droppings, then this could be the roost site of a tree creeper, which presses its tiny body into the trunk while it sleeps.

Of course very old, dead and decaying trees generally provide a mass of potential nest sites in addition to a well-stocked larder of insects and grubs, which are irresistible to most of the garden birds, particularly when they are feeding youngsters. Obviously, these trees are a very important food reservoir for wild birds and every effort should be made to retain old trees until they are finally too dangerous to be left standing.

However, during their final years the trees can be given a beneficial stay of execution if any large branches that look unstable are removed. When cutting off branches, always leave a short stub close to the trunk. When these are hollowed out with a small axe they provide excellent nest sites, especially if a strip of bark is nailed partially over the entrance so as to provide a hole or ledge nest site.

Holes can be drilled in the trunk of dead trees. Fill them with suet and you may be able to encourage woodpeckers to carry on with excavation and create their own nest site.

A tree creeper perfectly camouflaged in its favourite position close to the trunk of a tree

Improvised nest sites

Finally, on the subject of improvising nest sites, look around the garden – any hole or ledge has potential. Even that rickety old trellis supporting the roses can be reinforced with a few lengths of 5-centimetre square timber. Also, why not lay loose wire mesh over any trellis work? It will provide a good base for many types of nest and, if loosely fitted, will prevent the cat from visiting your avian guests.

Before getting involved in the practicalities of actually making your own nest boxes, explore ways of utilising everyday objects to provide potential nest sites. Take, for instance, that old kettle with the burnt-out element: ram it into a wall, shrub or tree, spout downwards to drain it, and it may well be taken up by wrens or robins, or even spotted flycatchers and blackbirds. Keeping the entrance clear of any twigs and branches will give it greater protection against the attention of four-legged predators such as mice and rats. I know that a kettle may not be aesthetically pleasing, so if in doubt, why not try a large flowerpot or half a coconut shell? Coconut shells can be cut in half then, with a few holes drilled for drainage, can be jammed into a sheltered bush or wall plant. Any type of cup may be used to create this type of nest site, provided, that is, there is good drainage. The coconut size could be used by spotted flycatchers, while larger cups may become the home of blackbirds, thrushes and robins.

Any large flower pot with a drainage hole of 2.8 centimetres can be hung from a post or a tree by a length of wire passed through a hole drilled in the rim of the pot. The weight of the pot will keep it firmly in position. This form of site is almost everlasting and has probably the most efficient drainage of any nest site. Coupled with this, the flower pot nest is protection against squirrels and other predators. In fact, the only danger to the nest is someone lifting the pot to investigate the contents – which will slide out with disastrous consequences. Pots are favourite nest sites of blue tits and great tits, who will also go in for a flower pot sited on a ledge or shelf.

While you are in the garden shed, why not see what other junk could be used as nest sites? The shed itself, providing there is an ever-open gap of about 15 centimetres square through which the birds can come and go, can be made home to many species, including swallows – that bundle of peasticks can be tied horizontally to the wall somewhere up near the ceiling. Swallows love this sort of site, as do robins and blackbirds. A wire cup moulded into the centre of the bundle would make the site more attractive to the two latter species. Similarly, if the bundle of sticks were stood on end in a corner, once again with a wire nest cup, the blackbirds may well raise one or two broods in it.

Blackbirds also appreciate an old basket fixed on the wall – the type designed to fit on the front of bicycles is an ideal size. An old seed tray nailed to the wall, near the ceiling, could also prove to be ideal for swallows and, of course, once again, blackbirds and robins.

Back outside, a simple tunnel site designed for wheatears in more remote areas could easily be adopted by robins and wagtails. Quite simply, place two standard bricks between two roof tiles on a bank, and camouflage all but the entrance with turves and branches. Once again, near the coast, these tunnels could be adopted by petrels.

The last type of improvised nest sites can be fashioned from scraps of wire netting. A simple, U-shaped mesh can be jammed into trees and shrubs where there are no naturally formed nest sites. Or mesh can provide a very effective nest platform, with the added benefit of unhindered drainage. It can also be made to different dimensions to suit all possible applications. The obvious species to adopt these, provided that they are well camouflaged and free from disturbance, are blackbirds and thrushes. However, if the platforms are fixed in a tree or bush that is over 3.5 metres above the ground, they may also interest mistle thrushes or wood pigeons. Sites similar to these have proved very successful in aviaries, particularly for foreign doves.

Nest boxes

Once any scope for improvisation is exhausted, then purpose-made nest boxes and ledges have to be bought or, preferably, made at home from pieces of wood. That's the beauty

The weasel can only be kept out of nest boxes with an inverted cone over the hole

of home-made nest boxes – there is no need to buy expensive timber and definitely no need to resort to the imported hardwoods which are causing so much environmental concern.

The improvisation at possible natural sites and the utilisation of tree holes may be superb methods of attracting wild birds, but the species involved are severely restricted to just a few types. Home-made nest boxes can be tailored in an attempt to attract species that have not previously nested in your garden or even in your locality.

But even if you have lovingly constructed a nest box to suit a particular species, always be prepared for the unpredictable whims of your visiting birds. More often than not, a different species will set up home in the nest box, with the birds you had hoped to attract settling nicely into a box designed for another. Wild birds are renowned for selecting what seems to us the most inappropriate of places to nest and will quite often nidificate on the roof of a nest box, spurning your invitation to go inside.

'Nidificate'? So wrote Revd F. O. Morris in *Morris's Nests and Eggs of British Birds*. It is a wonderful set of old books which, if I remember rightly, I obtained in a swap for a Dinky toy when I was much, much younger. The pages are beautifully produced and include details of British griffon and Egyptian vultures, spotted eagles and hawk owls. The point is, Revd Morris talks continually about nidification and never mentions 'nest-building'; they mean the same thing, but I promise not to use the word nidification again.

7 **A Home of Your Own**
or DIY Nest Boxes

Most wild birds are busy nesting from mid-April to the end of July, so it is important that nest boxes are erected well in advance, preferably by mid-February at the latest. They are very particular about their nest sites and will often spend a considerable time deliberating over the worth of a particular situation. A nest box fitted early ensures that there is plenty of time for the birds to decide. As usual, though, birds are unpredictable and some, especially blue tits, have been known to select a new nest box within 24 hours of it being erected.

Probably the best time to erect nest boxes is during the autumn and early winter months. This gives the birds ample opportunity to consider the site and become familiar with it. Some birds may even use these nest boxes for protection when roosting during winter.

Apart from the obvious requirements of safety and protection, a bird will also consider the space available in a nest box and whether there is enough room in which to house a nestful of well-grown youngsters together with their parent during the times of brood-ing. There must also be ample space to enable the young to exercise prior to leaving the nest.

Hole-nesting birds are likely to take into account the size of an entrance hole and whether it will admit the nesting pair while keeping out unwanted larger birds and predators. The nest box should not be placed anywhere that is likely to be either too hot or too cold. More specifically, it should not be exposed to full sunlight, as this can cause overheating and the subsequent death of all the inmates. The nest box will be more acceptable if it is in a dry and sheltered position and is fixed at a suitable height above the ground.

Once these conditions have been satisfied there is some chance that the nest box may be inhabited. These may seem impossible to fulfil, yet it is surprising the vast number of nest boxes that are used now that the hedge and woodland sites are being destroyed.

Materials for nest boxes
The materials used in the construction of nest boxes should be kept to those that are easily

worked, notably wood and roofing felt. The metal, plastic or composition types are more efficiently produced by the manufacturers and are best obtained from their distributors. Mind you, metal can be a problem in cold or hot weather.

Wood is cheap and easily available and can be worked with the minimum of tools and expertise. In fact, nest boxes made to a high standard of craftsmanship may well fail through lack of drainage and ventilation from the joints. This doesn't mean that the nest boxes should not be to a certain standard, for a reasonably well-made box will require less maintenance than one constructed from inferior components.

Soft woods are easy to use and will last for many years, provided that they are treated regularly with a good quality, organic, exterior wood preservative, preferably a water-based preservative such as Fenceguard. In fact, if the wood is acquired in its rough state, before it has been planed smooth, it will be even cheaper and will have absorbent qualities that will help keep the nest site free from moisture.

A particularly good stand-by for nest-box materials are old floorboards that can usually be obtained from one of the many house demolition sites around. The floorboards are generally of an ideal size, being 15 centimetres wide and are thick enough to provide insulation and security to the inmates of nest boxes.

Wooden nest boxes should all be made with

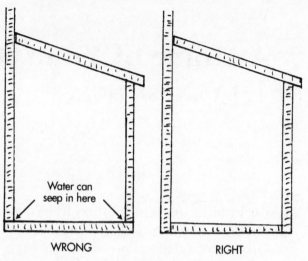

The right and wrong way to fit baseboards to nest boxes

the wood grain running downwards, as it greatly assists the dispersal of any rain. For similar reasons, there should be no exposed horizontal joints that may divert water into the box. The nest-box floor, in particular, should also be fitted inside the four walls.

Enclosed nest boxes should be fitted with inspection doors that can be either hinged or fitted flush to the top of the box. They should always be fitted with a hook and eye to prevent the accidental opening of a box by a predator. These doors are intended to make it possible to inspect the box at the end of the season (*not* while the box is occupied).

Hinged doors are the most convenient method of opening a nest box, provided that the hinges are not made of steel, which will rust and seize up after a short while. Brass or plastic hinges are durable alternatives, but may prove expensive and might also have a steel pin through them that could rust and prevent them from working.

Far more acceptable than all these hinges are home-made fittings that are both cheap and durable. Strips of leather or rubber can be fitted from the roof of the nest box to the back plate and fastened with most sorts of carpet tacks. These will last for many years and, if cut to cover the full width of the box, will form an added waterproof seal.

Pieces of roofing felt should be used to cover all nest boxes that are to be used in outdoor situations. Any boxes that are not water-proofed should only be used under cover, where they will not be subjected to wet weather.

When making and erecting nest boxes you should always look on the project as a long-term involvement, possibly for five years or more, or as long as a nest box is serviceable. Many boxes will not be taken during the first, second or even third year, but may eventually become so weathered and natural as to be attractive to a pair of birds previously too shy to nest in a man-made contrivance.

Having used a nest box once, many birds will return every year to the same spot. When they die, their offspring may carry on the tradition. This is especially the case with blue tit families. Any nest box that has been taken by a late-arriving migrant should be kept vacant until their probable return the follow-ing spring. This is easily achieved by blocking nest box entrances with rags until evidence of the migrants' return has been seen.

Do-it-yourself nest boxes can be separated into three basic types: 1) the wholly enclosed nest box with just a simple entrance hole of the right dimension; 2) a simple ledge, tray or raft, sometimes with a roof (ensure that the box is concealed in an appropriate position); and 3) a tunnel or chimney nest box, which principally has an extra long entrance cham-ber, and is more suitable for the larger owls.

Enclosed nest boxes

Most wooden nest boxes can be cut from one length of timber; the enclosed nest box, suit-able for a tit, can be cut from one length of timber, 147 centimetres long. It should be marked for cutting as shown.

With simple adjustments to the dimen-sions, the diagram can be applied to lengths of timber suitable for many sizes of nest box. When cutting wood for the roof and front it is

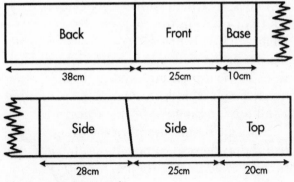

Cutting-sizes for a nest box

as well to cut at an angle to ensure better contact between them and a more weather-proof joint. Fixing the lengths of wood together does not require drilling and screwing, simple glue and nail joints are quite sufficient.

A few holes should always be drilled in the base to ensure adequate drainage and ventilation. Holes should also be drilled at opposite ends of the back plate to facilitate easier fixing to a tree, wall or post.

Particularly important, in the enclosed type of nest box, is the entrance hole. A difference of half a centimetre may mean that small birds can be evicted by larger and more aggressive birds, able to enter the nest box because of the added width of the entrance hole. House sparrows are well known for their harassing activities towards smaller birds and can be prevented from gaining access.

The round entrance holes can be precisely cut with a suitable sized hole-saw attachment for an electric drill. Alternatively, a jigsaw or keyhole saw would suffice, particularly for square or oval entrances.

The enclosed, tit-nest box is probably the most versatile of all designs. With simple variations to the dimensions and to the size of the entrance hole, this type of box can be adapted to suit a wide range of bird species.

The basic requirements of the design are to ensure that there is sufficient depth below the entrance hole, inside the box, to prevent any predators from reaching the contents of the

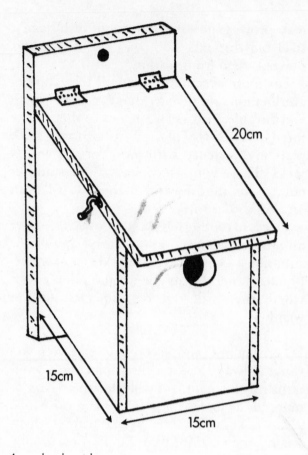

An enclosed nest box

nest itself. The roof should be fitted to overhang the entrance hole, once again to deter predators but also to give some protection from wet weather.

It must be stressed that on no account should perches be attached to this or any other nest box design. A perch will only provide predators and nuisances, such as jays,

Dimensions for hole nester boxes (in cm)

Species	back plate	sides	lid	front	entrance hole	floor area	floor to hole
Marsh Tit	35	25–27.5	20	25	2.5–2.8	10×10	17.5
Tree Swallow	37.5	25–27.5	20	25	2.8–3.1	10×10	17.5
Pied Flycatcher	37.5	25–27.5	20	25	3.1–3.8	10×10	17.5
Great Tit	37.5	25–27.5	20	25	2.8	10×10	17.5
Blue Tit	37.5	25–27.5	20	25	2.5–2.8	10×10	17.5
Nuthatch	37.5	25–27.5	20	25	2.8–3.8	10×10	17.5
Starling	50	37.5–40	30	37.5	5	22.5×22.5	30
House Sparrow	42.5	30–32.5	22.5	30	3.8	15×15	22.5
Wren	37.5	25–27.5	20	25	5	10×10	17.5
Green Woodpecker	57.5	45–47.5	22.5	45	6.25	12.5×12.5	37.5
Great Spotted Woodpecker	50	37.5–40	22.5	37.5	5	12.5×12.5	30
Black Redstart	37.5	25–27.5	20	25	3.8	10×10	17.5
Wryneck	37.5	25–27.5	22.5	25	3.8–4.3	12.5×12.5	17.5
Willow Tit	37.5	25–27.5	20	25	2.8	10×10	17.5
Coal Tit	37.5	25–27.5	20	25	2.5–2.8	10×10	17.5
Created Tit	37.5	25–27.5	20	25	2.8–3.8	10×10	17.5
Tree Creeper	37.5	25–27.5	20	25	3.8	10×10	17.5
Redstart	25	27.5–30	22.5	27.5	2.8–5	12.5×12.5	20
Hoopoe	50	37.5–40	30	37.5	5	22.5×22.5	30
Jackdaw	65	50–55	45	50	15	35×35	42.5
Ring-necked Parakeet	50	37.5–40	30	37.5	5	22.5×22.5	30

magpies and sparrows, with a ready-built foothold on which to perch and harass the occupants. All hole-nesting birds are agile enough to enter and leave the nest site without the need of assistance.

Entrance holes should always be cut into the front of the box, beneath the overhang of the roof. This positioning is designed to deter four-legged predators who might otherwise have been able to reach the nest while holding on to the tree or post to which the box is fixed. The table lists some of the species likely to use the enclosed nest box, together with the different dimensions and characteristics favoured by those species. As is always the case with wild birds, other species which are not listed may adopt this type of nest box, and some of those listed may choose other types.

The columns numbered one to six detail the sizes required when marking up and cutting the timber, column seven gives the minimum recommended interior height from the floor to the bottom lip of the entrance hole. This height must be maintained in order to allow any fledglings room for exercise and reaching the hole, whilst guaranteeing that they will be safe from squirrels and other predators, who could otherwise reach in through the entrance. There should always be a minimum distance of 18 centimetres below the entrance.

These recommendations are not a guarantee of fulfilling the needs of a bird species, but are more of a general guide. Should there be any danger of interference by people, the boxes should be fixed at a minimum height of 3.5 metres above the ground, preferably with no branches nearby that would assist an enterprising climber.

Wedge-shaped nest boxes

The wedge-shaped box has been introduced primarily to attract tree creepers, whose natural nest sites – in crevices or in the bark of old and decaying trees – have been either destroyed or replaced with inhospitable conifers.

The nest boxes can be fitted to tree trunks at practically any height, there is apparently no position that is a particular favourite. Irregularities in the trunk should be removed

prior to fixing and the back plate fitted on, for which even a patch of bark is suitable.

When constructing a wedge-type box, it is absolutely essential to adhere to the instructions and only allow a 5-centimetre hole on each side. When the back plate is fitted, it effectively reduces the size to 3 centimetres. With the holes maintained at this size, the box may also be used by coal tits, blue tits and tree sparrows. Any entrance larger than this will admit the house sparrow, who will effectively end any occupation by a smaller bird.

Instead of drainage holes, as in conventional nest boxes, it will be necessary to cut some notches in the base of the front panel to

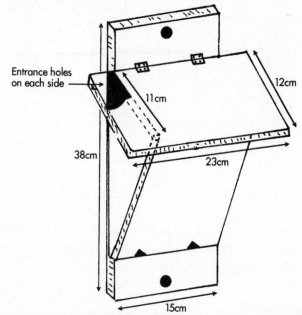

Entrance holes on each side

12cm

11cm

38cm

23cm

15cm

A wedge-shaped nest box

allow any water that might collect to flow out.

Tree creepers are delightful little birds and show a marked degree of tameness when searching for food from tree to tree. However, in the nest, they are extremely nervous and will desert at the slightest intrusion. For this reason absolute care must be taken when inspecting the nest. In fact, it is better not to visit the site at all.

Tree creeper nest boxes
Another nest box, designed for tree creepers, and which has proved to be very successful on the Continent, is made from rough timber, with roofing felt for the top and bottom – making it extremely easy to put together. Two pieces of wood are glued and nailed at 90° to one another. The roofing felt is then tacked to the top and bottom and, using the tree as a template, is cut to fit the curve of the trunk. The entrance slits, one on each side, should be 5 centimetres wide and 2 centimetres deep.

Fixing to the tree can either be done with two pieces of wire or with four screws.

Another type of tree creeper nest box can be made from any log of a suitable width. It is first cut into four segments. The inside is hollowed out to provide as much space as possible. An entrance hole 5 centimetres deep and 2.5 centimetres wide is cut and all the sections are fitted together. The lid and the base are then cut from similar logs of wood and fitted to the box.

Although very pleasing when completed,

A swift cannot take off from the ground and has to launch itself from buildings

the making of the box is time-consuming and it deteriorates rapidly. All in all, it has been found to be inferior to the wedge-shaped box. If it *is* used, it should be fixed to the underside of sloping branches.

Nests for swifts

The swift, although generally associated with swallows and martins, has completely different nesting habits. Firstly, being a somewhat larger bird, it requires more room for nesting than could be found in a simple mud cup. Designed for an aerial life, it is incapable of landing on the ground and taking off. This makes it impossible for the swift to collect mud for nest-building as do the swallows and martins. Instead, it has adapted itself to nest in holes, conveniently in the top of high buildings.

The sloping nest box is designed specifically for swifts and should be fixed as high as possible on a building, preferably directly under the eaves.

The entrance hole should be 2.5 centimetres deep and 5 centimetres wide. To encourage nesting, a ring of twisted straw should be placed inside, as far from the entrance as possible. The swifts will add their own nest material – feathers and other flotsam, gathered on the wing and cemented together with saliva, rather like the nests of related Indo-Australian swifts – which are used for bird's-nest soup, that great favourite of the Orient. Mind you, knowing the parasite infestation of the poor swift, I must admit that I would be reluctant to partake of this so-called delicacy.

Swifts will nest in the highest possible situations, even above 25 metres on some of the taller buildings and churches. The rectangular swift-nest box has been found to be very successful fixed at heights from 6 to 25 metres. Like the other swift boxes, these should be fitted immediately under the roof of a building, particularly under the eaves to which they can be tailored to fit. The boxes can be fitted from the outside with hooks to facilitate removal for cleaning.

Fitting the boxes this way makes it very awkward to gain access for cleaning. A more convenient method is to cut a hole in the roof edges, directly over the inspection doors. The boxes can then be reached from inside the roof space, obviating the need for their removal every time access is required.

In a similar manner to that recommended for the wedge-shaped swift box, a ring of straw should be placed inside the box, approximately 30 centimetres from the entrance hole underneath.

This form of nest site is unfortunately very well favoured by house sparrows and starlings who will, if allowed, be in possession when the swifts arrive in May from their migration. In view of this it is necessary to block the entrance hole until the swifts arrive – by this time the house sparrows and starlings will have found alternative accommodation.

Seed-tray nests

A structure similar to the simple seed-tray nest site is the swallow nest ledge. This can be fitted to the interior walls of an outbuilding, provided that there is always access for the nesting birds. Swallows favour this type of nest site when it is fitted high up, close to the roof of the building.

Always hang old sacking or polythene sheeting below the nest site to protect the surrounding area from the young swallows' copious droppings.

Swallows, like the swifts, are late in arriving in this country and may find that their nest ledges have been acquired by blackbirds, robins or wrens. As this nest site is so simple to create it would not be a hardship to produce one or two more to replace those taken by the other birds. Swallows, while preferring to nest inside buildings or beneath porches, do not object to more than one nesting pair being under the same roof.

Swallow nest cups

Another type of site that can be introduced is the swallow nest cup, mounted on to a board for easy fixing. This nest cup can be fashioned from builder's plaster or baked clay, moulded around a 23-centimetre rubber ball.

The empty site should be kept free from sparrows until the swallows arrive back in this country. Once again, it must be stressed that access to sites should be open at all times.

Nests for house martins

House martins are similar to swifts and swallows, only visiting the British Isles during the summer. Their nest preferences are different from the swifts and swallows in that they build their nests on the outside of buildings and build their cup-shaped nests entirely of mud. Like the swifts, they nest as high as possible under the eaves of barns and houses.

It is possible to make artificial house martin nests that can be fitted under the eaves of a building, but it is very doubtful that they can be anything like the quality of the commercially available cups that are made from a cement composition.

The most practical way to make a house martin nest-cup is to use a child's 23-centimetre rubber ball as a mould. Around one quarter of the ball, masked with cardboard, should be applied a liberal coat of builder's plaster. A small gap, 7.5 by 2 centimetres should be left, in the top edge, to serve as an entrance hole. Once the plaster has set it can be mounted on to two pieces of wood with more plaster to hold it securely. The two pieces of wood should be butted together at right angles. This whole assembly can then be fitted under the eaves of a building with four cup hooks that allow for removal of the nest for cleaning.

Artificial nests will probably not prompt the setting up of a new house martin colony, but they will increase the available nest sites in established situations. Martins, once established, will return to the same site every year.

House martins have always been pestered by house sparrows, who often take over the martins' nests and evict both eggs and young. A novel method of controlling this menace has been thought up, based on the principle that house martins can approach their nests at a much steeper angle than can sparrows.

About 15 centimetres in front of the nest is hung a row of lengths of string with tiny brass nuts tied on to keep them taut. The string should be cut to lengths of 33 centimetres and be fixed at 6-centimetre intervals. Provided that all the pieces of string are of the same length, they will not tangle and they will effectively allow house martins to reach the nest but prevent sparrows from doing so.

Nest tray with roof

When fixed at over 2 metres from the ground and camouflaged with leaves and branches, this site, shown below, proves attractive to blackbirds and thrushes.

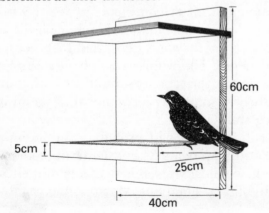

Birch-log nest boxes

Lengthy discussions have taken place among bird lovers on the merits of the silver birch-log nest box. Doubt has been cast on the aesthetic value of a birch box mounted on any tree other than a birch. Birds obviously take not the slightest notice of where the box is mounted. Their only concern is the suitability of the site with regard to safety and practicality.

The making of the birch-log nest box is probably best left to the manufacturers with the correct equipment for boring out the centre of the wood to the required diameter. It is essential that there is enough space inside a box for a pair of blue tits to raise their considerable families. The centre space should be at least 9.5 centimetres in diameter, with a 17.5-centimetre drop from the entrance hole to the floor. Generally, the birch-log nest box is a modification of the enclosed nest box and dimensions detailed in the table can likewise be applied to these boxes.

One important consideration is that there must be good drainage as the birch nest box is susceptible to waterlogging, usually with disastrous effects on the inmates. Good drainage will also slow down the rotting process of the birch log.

Hollow-branch nest boxes

The hollow-branch nest box has been found to be very successful in attracting redstarts to nest. It is constructed from the hollow branch

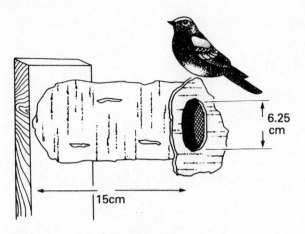

Hollow branch used by redstarts

of an old tree and positioned 2 metres from the ground. Other hollow branches may be used and, because of the protection from predators, may encourage other species of hole nesters.

The mounting should be improvised to suit a particular log. However, a metal plate, fixed to the log, and then screwed to a post, has proved to be most satisfactory.

Open-front nest boxes

The open-front nest box is very popular with many species and if placed in suitable places it may well attract species that would, generally, never use an artificial nest site. If the box is mounted near to a fast-flowing stream it may be used by grey wagtails or a slightly larger box may even be attractive to a pair of dippers. Spotted flycatchers and pied wagtails often use this type of nest box, particularly if it is mounted in an exposed position away from disturbance.

The list of birds favouring open-fronted sites is long and includes robins, redstarts, black redstarts, house sparrows, great and blue tits and even wrens.

One pitfall with this type of nest site is that it is very liable to predation, especially by jays and magpies. This does discourage many birds from nesting and should be taken into consideration when deciding which types of nest boxes you wish to erect.

Square-holed nest boxes

The square-holed nest box is a combination of the enclosed and the open fronted boxes. Consequently, the dimensions listed in the table should be applied to this nest box; the only alteration being the excavation of a square hole rather than a round one.

Species, other than those shown in the table, that may use large, square-holed nest boxes include stock doves, little owls, goldeneyes, mandarins, tawny owls and kestrels.

Should a tall tree have a suitable fork into which a triangular version of the enclosed box could be fitted, then one should be made, similar to the drawing on p. 98. The design has proved very successful for nesting birds, and the whole box is very picturesque, especially when painted in dovecote white.

The dimensions are self-explanatory and can be adjusted to suit any situations, the entrance hole, however, should be retained at 17.5 by 12.5 centimetres.

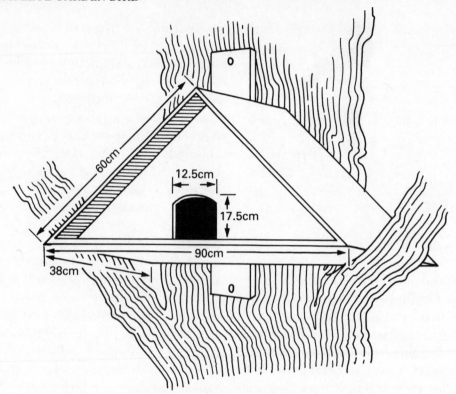

60cm

12.5cm

17.5cm

90cm

38cm

Triangular enclosed square-holed nest box

Although originally designed for stock doves, this type of box has been used frequently by owls, kestrels and jackdaws. It must be sited over 6 metres above the ground.

Mallard boxes
Designed to be made from very rough timber, the mallard box is probably too large for many gardens, but some people are lucky enough to have mallards visiting who may well take to this duck box. The box is intended

to allow the sitting bird all round vision through the cracks between the panels.

The best situation for this nest box is on a small raft, anchored in position. This not only allows the nest site to float on rising water but also prevents many predators making a meal of the large quantity of eggs laid by mallards.

The boxes should be taken in at the end of a season and thoroughly cleaned and dried. Before being set out the following year, they should be treated with a good, water-based wood preservative, once again not containing toxic chemicals.

As you can see, the variety and scope of home-made nest boxes can seem mind-bogglingly endless. Deciding which type to try may seem a daunting task, but by acquiring a copy of your *County Bird Report*, from your local library, you will get some idea of which species you may attract and then can decide just where to fix all those desirable residences.

Timing

Many factors affect the erection of nest boxes. In particular, the time of year must be chosen so that the birds will not be perturbed by unfamiliar objects being set out in their territories. During the autumn, most birds are more intent on feeding to sustain them for either the winter or for migration. This is the most suitable time for erecting boxes, allowing the resident birds the whole winter in which to become accustomed to the new boxes.

Siting

The siting of nest boxes is particularly important and you should note the preferences of wild birds outside the garden environment. Most garden birds have evolved from woodland species and it will be seen that these birds in the wild only nest in light situations in the trees and shrubs at the edge away from the dark centres of the wood.

The larger woodland birds nest high in the canopy, once again in a light situation away from the dark centre. Birds will not tolerate dark surroundings to their nest, even though the inside of the nest itself might be a pitch-black hole. This must be taken into account when deciding where to place the nest sites.

Wild birds usually build their nests within certain height tolerances; many, particularly blackbirds, robins and wrens prefer to nest only a metre or so from the ground. Careful consideration should be given to these preferences and, once again, every effort should be made to re-create the natural characteristics.

Wild birds have different characteristics when it comes to living and feeding within close proximity to others of the same species. The nest boxes of aggressive species such as tits and robins should be kept apart, with a maximum of two to four boxes per acre as the limit of their tolerances. Colonially nesting birds; martins, starlings, sparrows, petrels and other sea birds, will all choose to nest close to each other. Some dominant species should be kept completely apart or they may jeopardise any hopes of other birds nesting. For instance, a kestrel or owl nest would probably make most small birds move to other sites.

When the anticipated territories have been sorted and the proposed sites confirmed, the boxes can be fixed in their permanent positions on walls, trees or posts. A nest box should always be tilted forward, very slightly, to offer some protection from sun and rain.

Care must be taken to avoid the drainage channels, particularly when fixing boxes to trees. Excessive rain is always naturally guided down the same channels on most trees and is often marked by a green strip. Any nest box obstructing the water flow would soon become flooded.

A tree with low growth and branches should always be avoided, as predators will find it much easier to climb to the nest site. A tree with no growth below the proposed nest site is far more suitable and is preferred by most birds for the safety offered from concealed enemies. Elm trees have a very rough bark that is easily climbed by predators and should not be used as a nest tree.

Securing

There are several ways of fixing nest boxes to the trunks of trees. The most secure fixing is with 7.5 centimetre screws. Although steel screws are susceptible to rust, they can be protected with a coat of Vaseline before they are driven in. Using screws ensures that the boxes can be easily removed if necessary.

Steel nails can be used but are very likely to snap should an attempt be made to remove them. Should this occur in trees that are eventually to be felled as timber, damage can be caused to saw blades in the milling process. Copper nails would not cause damage at saw mills but are rather expensive and likely to bend when being hammered in.

The latest method of fixing boxes to trees is with tapered wooden pegs that are forced into previously drilled holes, both in the box and in the tree. These are proving to be very successful and should, in future, always be considered when boxes or signs need to be fixed to trees.

The only way of fixing boxes to trees without causing immediate damage is with wire bands wrapped around the box and the trunk of the tree. Damage will only occur when the tree grows larger and the wire bands are too small to encircle the enlarged girth without cutting into the trunk. Eventually, the wire will cause deformity in the tree and may also cause its death. This disaster can be avoided by annual adjustment of the size of the wire.

Nest boxes should be fixed to walls and buildings with Rawlplugs and screws. The masonry is first drilled with a hardened-tip drill, and a Rawlplug inserted. The box is then fixed with steel screws, once again covered in Vaseline. This method, although long-winded, does allow the boxes to be removed if they are unsuccessful; simple fixing with masonry nails has to be regarded as more or less permanent.

Should there be a shortage of suitable trees to hold nest boxes, they can be fixed to posts firmly embedded in the ground. The timber used should be 10 centimetres square and the pole a minimum of 2 metres above the ground.

Inspection

Consideration could be given, when erecting the nest boxes, to the ease with which the contents could be examined. Ornithologists have divided views on this subject. Some say it is necessary to record the sizes of broods etc., while others insist that this isn't necessary. The opening of nest boxes to inspect the contents can upset the parent birds and lead to desertion of the eggs or young. Although this is not always the case the risk of disturbance seems a good reason not to bother the birds and their nest. The nuthatch and the tree creeper, in particular, and many other species will definitely desert if their boxes are interfered with. Any bird that is disturbed during the evening or night is unlikely to return to the nest until dawn, by which time the eggs or young would be fatally chilled.

Nest materials

Once the nest boxes are in position, it sometimes encourages potential nesters if some leaves or dry grass are scattered inside them. Provision of nest materials in the vicinity is always worthwhile and can be arranged by putting suitable materials in wire mesh baskets that can be hung on branches or laid on the ground. Suitable materials that the nesting birds would collect are sheep's wool, small down feathers, dry oak and beech leaves and short dog's hair. Cotton wool tends to tangle and is not recommended as potential nest materials. Nor are lengths of cotton. Nest materials are greatly appreciated by the birds and possibly play a major part in keeping pairs together in the vicinity for nesting.

Once the hen bird is involved in nest building, her natural instincts prepare her for egg laying, which occurs when the work on the nest is nearly completed. She will probably lay only one egg per day and will not start to brood them until the whole clutch is laid. This is one of the reasons why cold eggs that are in a nest are not necessarily dead and should not be removed.

Maintenance

During the autumn all nest boxes should be opened and cleaned thoroughly with boiling water and a ten per cent ammonia solution that will destroy all the parasites and their eggs, which invariably are left behind when the birds leave. When emptying a box, always search carefully through the old nest material in case some of the bird's eggs have been overlooked and will never hatch.

Any drainage holes should be cleaned out with wire and re-drilled if necessary. When the boxes are thoroughly cleaned, leave them opened for a few weeks to allow air to circulate and freshen them up.

During the winter months, look out for any birds that use empty boxes for roosting. Mice and dormice are very fond of spending the winter in bird boxes and may be encouraged to stay and breed if alternative accommodation is prepared for the birds.

8 What's That Bird?

As a consequence of working with wild bird casualties, I meet all manner of species, most of which I can identify straight off. There are still some, though, that catch me out because they bear no resemblance to those two-dimensional reproductions in bird identification manuals. This may be because, like many men, I suffer from a degree of colour-blindness, particularly with the red, green and brown combinations that are such a part of identifying small garden birds.

Size also plays an important part in identification, but simply being told a bird's measurements is often not much help. We may be told that a bird is 9 centimetres, 14 centimetres or even 16.5 centimetres long; but can *you* tell the difference between 14 and 16.5 centimetres of bird fleeting across your lawn?

To make my life easier, especially with free-flying birds, I start my identification by comparing the size of my subject with a bird species familiar to me. In my mind it's no good resorting to inches or centimetres, even if we could make up our national mind whether or not we had gone metric.

Everyone, for instance, can visualise the size of the ubiquitous house sparrow, but how many people realise that the tree sparrow, dunnock, robin, meadow pipit, the wagtails and the lesser spotted woodpecker, all appear to be about the same size?

Sparrows and others

At this point, I ought to give some more details about sparrows and some clues on how to identify the two common species. Yes, there are two species: the one we all know and love to have living around our homes, the house sparrow; and the only slightly smaller tree sparrow. Any all-brown, nondescript sparrow with no black bib is a female house sparrow. The two sexes of the tree sparrow are similar but can be separated from the male house sparrow by their chestnut coloured crowns, as opposed to the cock house sparrow's grey; and also the black mark on the cheeks of the tree sparrows will assist those who, like me, are colour blind.

Having visualised your sparrow, and using size as the first yardstick, or metrestick, divide the various birds you see into groups. Some will be obviously distinctive, while others – the pipits, buntings and dunnocks – will all look remarkably alike, especially on a dreary winter's day when they are all likely to visit your feeding station. Then is the time to apply the next criterion for identification: 'jizz'. This is probably a new word to those outside serious birdwatching circles but it is absolutely essential if you want to confirm a bird just by a fleeting glimpse or even in silhouette against a dawn sky.

My dictionary has no entry for the word 'jizz', but to me it describes the general countenace of a bird, how it holds itself and how it moves. It can even be loosely applied to where in the garden the bird is likely to be seen and what it's likely to be doing.

Let's take another small, brown, sparrow-sized bird – the tree creeper – and look at it as a moving, elusive garden bird. All you will see is a small, brown, sparrow-sized bird climbing to the top of the trunk of the tree like a little mouse, then flying down to the bottom of the next tree and climbing that trunk, and so on, tree after tree, always climbing upwards. Only a tree creeper would behave like this, for the only other bird that clings and climbs close to the tree trunks is the nuthatch – a bird that is only slightly larger but with a grey back instead of a brown one, and it will travel both *up* and *down* the trunk, often descending head

A baby blackbird, with far less 'jizz' than its mother, even though at first glance, they may look the same

first, which is unheard of in a tree creeper.

Jizz familiarity is also, probably, the most useful method of identifying juvenile birds just before they get their adult plumage. During the summer months we take in hundreds of supposedly orphaned blackbirds with juvenile plumage of dark-brown feathers speckled with light tips. Most of these are described by their rescuers as thrushes merely because they are speckled whereas, in fact, a thrush – from first feathers to adulthood – has only a speckled chest, which comprises dark spots on a very pale background. Also, a young blackbird sits much squarer than a young song thrush, which tends to perch with its head in the air. It's difficult to describe perfectly, it's just jizz.

Then, of course, there is dimorphism – the difference between the sexes of a species – which often leaves many of the females, which are naturally dowdy so as to be unobtrusive on the nest, looking like other species or even their own growing offspring. Surely none of us could mistake the cock blackbird, with his golden beak and golden eye? But look at the female: brown and drab, with none of her mate's finery; though she still has his proud bearing and somehow looks different from a fully grown youngster – jizz again.

The third identifying feature of any bird, although more prominent in males, could be called 'jazz' – the sounds, both musical and tone deaf, made by different species. I have always accepted that there are three master songsters in or around the garden: the blackbird, with his beautiful fluted tones; the song thrush, with his slightly more treble oft-repeated phrases; and the nightingale, with his beautiful, clear midnight echoes. In my bird books, and on the television, they all look roughly the same size, but take a closer look at the small print – the blackbird and the song thrush are indeed about the same size (25 and 23 centimetres respectively), but the nightingale is tiny; at 16 centimetres it is hardly bigger than a robin. It is easily separated from the robin because it does not have the latter's obvious red chest; but what if you compared the nightingale with a robin-sized garden warbler that has similar, subtle colours with, as my identification book puts it, 'no distinguishing features'? In this situation you would have to resort to identifying the different song patterns – the nightingale warbles much stronger notes.

I do not think it's practical to describe the '*pstees*' or '*ssips*' or '*little bit of bread and no chee-eese*' calls attributed to different species – you will only become familiar with these by actually listening to different songs and comparing them with the many records, tapes and compact discs available containing all manner of bird songs. Take, for instance, '*the little bit of bread and no chee-eese*' of the yellow-hammer. The song doesn't really sound a bit like that, but you can almost guarantee that any sparrow-sized yellow bird whistling its head off on the topmost sprig of a roadside bush will be the cock yellowhammer trying for the slightly less yellow female. Unfortunately, the yellowhammer will not make many excursions into the garden, except in very severe weather, when it may come in with its cousin, the reed bunting. The reed bunting in winter plumage looks just like a sparrow, except for the former's white collar and white moustache. Look at a reed bunting and watch its behaviour. It will look like a sparrow but then somehow you will know that it is different: it will not attempt to go on the bird table; it will not be in a gang and it will not be as boisterous or as bold as a sparrow. It will probably make no sound, so if you cannot see that white collar and moustache, it's only its jizz that will make it stand out from the crowd, and the fact that there is snow on the ground.

Really bad weather may be a time to expect a reed bunting to visit, but some birds follow a much broader seasonal routine – especially the migrants. It's much easier in the winter to identify birds when there are far fewer migrants in the garden to confuse you. Any migrants around are once again only likely to visit in really bad weather. By winter migrants I mean those that are in Britain between October and March, but remember that these dates are always flexible and try not to stick too rigidly to our calendar. Species only likely to be seen in winter include redwings, fieldfares, waxwings, bramblings and, possibly, some of the northern buntings such as the Lapland and snow buntings – both very rare visitors to bird tables.

In the summer it is a different picture, with many different species arriving to confuse you – from the many warblers to swallows, martins and swifts, to the two species of flycatcher and the inevitable cuckoos, well-known for their call but resembling a fat sparrowhawk in plumage and flight.

Perhaps the most obvious of the summer visitors, but still very rare in this country, is the hoopoe, unmistakable with its deep pink plumage, black and white wings and large pink crest tipped with black, quite unlike any other bird you are likely to see. I must say I cannot resist the written description of a hoopoe's call – it goes 'pooop-pooop-pooop' and has been described as sounding like a dog barking in the next street.

Having set down some rough guidelines to note, I ought to explain how I set about more systematic identification. Most bird books are set out in a regular, scientific and taxonomic order, starting with *Gaviiformes* (the divers) and finishing with the *Emberizidae* (the buntings). I shall avoid Latin names, and keep things simple starting with the smallest birds likely to visit the garden, working through to the larger, occasional visitors like owls and hawks.

Wrens

Some of the most familiar garden birds are in fact the smallest and, if I describe them all as wren-sized, I am sure you will soon be able to pick them out of a crowd. The wren itself, of course, is a tiny brown bird with no distinguishing marks, but just take a look at its jizz: this is the little bundle of feathers that climbs in and out of the lowest hedge branches; it will discreetly work its way up inside any climbers, and look for its favourite spider delicacies underneath the ledges and windowsills. It always carries its tail bolt upright in the air and if a bird literally scolds you from the cover of a bush it will be a wren; you will be amazed at just how loud that scolding will be.

The tit family

The blue tit surely needs no description. It will be on your peanut bags or raiding your bottles of milk. It's tiny and blue. There is no other bird like it as the only other tiny tit you will see in the garden is the coal tit, which has a bold black cap and bib with no blue, although it does have a white patch on the nape of the neck to distinguish it from the marsh and willow tits, unlikely garden visitors. In Scotland, gardens may entertain the crested tit which, as its name suggests, has a pronounced crest that is speckled and a black pair of sideburns but, once again, no blue.

The goldcrest and firecrest are those tiny birds with golden flashes on their foreheads. They probably will not visit your birdtable, but listen for their high-pitched contact calls in any fir trees. It is a single-syllable, oft-repeated 'see' or 'zit' and, far more than size or colour, is their most distinguishing feature.

There is another tit whose body is probably smaller than a wren's but whose very long tail makes it look larger. Aptly named, the long-tailed tit will pass through in small groups, swinging in and out of the higher branches of trees. Markedly black-and-white, you cannot possibly confuse it with any other bird, and its nearest look-alike is the larger, sparrow-sized wagtail, who wouldn't be seen dead swinging in a tree. (See p. 108 for great tits.)

Blue tits will make short work of your garden's aphid population, not to mention the nuts you put out

Wagtails

The wagtails, to me, appear sparrow-sized, although the bird books describe them at 18 centimetres, twenty-five per cent larger than a sparrow. They omit to mention that this extra 4 centimetres is all tail. All the species of wagtail that you are likely to meet, the pied, grey and yellow, have long tails which their owners constantly bob up and down as they walk rapidly around on the ground searching for insects. Colour is the important way of discriminating between the wagtails, although the yellow will be seen only during the summer. It is strikingly yellow all over with a greenish back, whereas the grey only has a yellow underneath with a dark, blue-grey back. This one is resident all year, as is the self-explanatory black-and-white, pied wagtail, by far the commonest of the three, although a greyer variety, the so-called 'white' variety, may appear as a visitor from mainland Europe.

Flycatchers

The grey wagtail may be spotted leaping to catch flying insects but with its colour it could never be confused with the master insect catcher, the spotted flycatcher. This is a brown, sparrow-sized bird that often nests in gardens. Identify this bird by its habit of sitting on a post making constant forays into the air to catch flying insects and then returning to its post. This is only a summer visitor but one that I can sit and watch for hours, marvelling at its aerobatic agility as it floats to and from its hawking post.

Its cousin, the pied flycatcher, is another summer visitor that is far less common, restricting itself to nesting locally in deciduous woodland towards the west of Britain. Its perching habit and shorter tail make it easy to separate from the pied wagtail. The female is, unfortunately, not so black-and-white but tends to be a more grey-brown colour, though it can be distinguished from the spotted flycatcher because it has no speckling on its bib or chest.

Dunnocks

As casualties come in to the hospital I can differentiate between the spotted flycatcher and the very similar dunnock by the former's more robust, blackish bill. However, in the garden the dunnock, formerly erroneously called the hedge sparrow, will usually be seen hopping on the ground, avidly searching for small insects in the low vegetation of hedge and plant bottoms. Its very thin, delicate bill singles it out as an insectivore quite different from the genuine sparrows with their massive crushing beaks.

Great tits

One size up from wren-sized birds are the sparrow-sized birds, which make up the bulk of the garden visitors. There is a sparrow-sized tit, the great tit, which will be a regular visitor to most peanut-holders. Its jizz is so obviously that of a tit as it performs acrobatics to get at the peanuts, but even if size does not give it away, the bright yellow chest and abdomen, with bold, black stripe down it merging into a handsome black bib and black cap, should leave you in no doubt as to its pedigree.

Warblers

Despite its matching headgear, the blackcap, another garden visitor, is easily distinguishable from the great tit by its body colouring – a greyish-brown back with a very pale chest and abdomen. However, its black cap does help to distinguish it from the other common warblers, summer visitors who all look alike. In fact, the only way to separate some species is by their song. In garden warblers, for instance, the song can be quite beautiful, but in grasshopper warblers it can be as monotonous as a cricket. Identifying warblers is an art in itself, although some have identifying colours, like the whitethroat – but, confusingly, not the lesser whitethroat, which is about the same size though without 'the greyish-wash on the chest'.

Apart from some very beautiful songs, warblers, birds of the bushes not the bird table, are fairly dull. Possibly the only excitement comes when some blackcaps stay throughout the winter, joining our only other resident warbler, the much-lauded but extremely rare Dartford warbler of the Dorset and Surrey heathlands, which you won't see in the garden.

Even a spotted flycatcher will stop for the occasional cup of tiny mealworms

Blackcap and caterpillars

Finches

One type of bird that you will see is the finch, and you will be able to tell one species from another easily. Finches are, in the main, very similar to sparrows in that they have fairly large bills which are designed by evolution for cracking and opening seeds. Mind you, each different type of finch seems to have a bill that is geared to a specific purpose; in fact, it was the subtle differences in the beaks of Galapagos finches in the Pacific that unlocked the secrets of evolution to Charles Darwin in the nineteenth century.

A greenfinch's beak is very similar to a sparrow's and just as powerful. The bird is not only very green, but it also has a tremendous amount of obvious yellow, especially on the wings, which can be seen as it flies to and from the peanut holder. Put out peanuts and you will attract greenfinches. You can also recognise them by what I describe as warbling-call notes. If you put your peanuts out in one of those red plastic bags, you may also attract a recent newcomer to the garden-bird scene, another finch: the siskin. Also very yellow, it is easy to tell from the greenfinch by its smaller size, smaller beak and also lack of green.

The other finch that will give you flashes of yellow feathers is the goldfinch, the most delicate of the finches, with a fine beak used to tweak the small seeds out of teasel and thistle heads. Although I believe colour is one of the less important criteria for identifying birds, the goldfinch just has to be described in terms of colour: its black wings heavily barred with gold, its black cap and bright red face make it handsome enough to vie with some of the exotic birds to be seen in tropical gardens. It is unlikely to visit the bird table, but a flock of goldfinches, known as a 'charm', may well descend on the seed heads of your herbaceous border, even if you do not grow thistles and teasels specifically to attract them.

Unlike the gregarious goldfinch, the most common finch, the chaffinch, will only be seen in pairs. A handsome bird with bold, white

This starling survived in the wild with a grossly overgrown beak

wingstripes that are particularly noticeable when the bird is flying, the chaffinch is a regular visitor to bird tables, being very fond of the small seed we feed to our canaries and budgerigars. In the breeding season the cock bird sprouts a deep pink chest and neck that is not dissimilar to the striking colouring of the bullfinch, the other regular garden visitor from the family. However, the bullfinch can be separated from the chaffinch by its black cap and short, stubby beak, which has evolved to allow the bird to eat buds and fruit. When it is flying it has noticeable dark wings and a vivid white rump.

The peanut-loving greenfinch

The most delicate of finches, the goldfinch

Martins, swallows and swifts

A white rump is also an easy way to tell flying house martins from the very similar swallows and swifts. However, apart from that, and if you have some experience of these three species, you will know that the swallow has a long, forked tail, whilst the swift has hardly any tail. Instead, it has long, thin wings held at right angles to its body. House martins chitter-chatter to each other as they rough and tumble, turning all sorts of somersaults to catch flying insects. Swallows perform lightning-fast sweeps to catch their prey, particularly over water, whereas the swifts feed much higher in the sky and seem to revel in being able to fly around gleefully, in small groups, flashing in-between our houses, screaming their *joie de vivre*, a wonderful sight on a warm summer's evening before they spiral up to the clouds to roost at goodness knows how many thousand feet.

Robins

Although it may look larger, the robin is also what I would call a sparrow-sized bird, though its longer legs give it the *appearance* of being more than the requisite 14 centimetres. Unfortunately, you will see only one or, at the most, two adult robins in your garden at one time as they are fiercely territorial and will attack, with the intention of killing, any other red breast which enters that territory. A resident robin will even attack a bundle of red feathers if you want to put it to the test. Only when a submissive female ventures upon the scene will there be more than one, and only then will more than one robin follow you as you carry out any gardening or even visit your kitchen – robins are notorious in their trust of human company.

Redstarts

The robin stands erect on its long thin legs just like the redstart, a summer visitor to some gardens. But there the similarity ends. The redstart may have a redbreast but it gets its name from its red tail, its 'start'. Other than that, it has a dusky-grey back fronted by a bold black face which is continued in the black redstart to cover most of its chest and abdomen. The black redstart, unheard of as a town-breeding bird before the 1939–45 War, afterwards found many of the London bomb-damaged buildings much to its liking as breeding territory.

Joining the black redstart, and taking advantage of man's buildings both bomb-damaged and whole, is the model for the next size of garden bird – the starling.

Starlings

The starling. Do we all recognise it? I am sure that most of us do, except when a juvenile turns up on your doorstep. True, the juvenile

The larvae of this crane fly – leather jackets – are favourite food of starlings

struts around like the adult, often following its parents, calling for food, but there the similarity ends – an adult starling is usually blackish in colour with green and purple iridescences setting off the whitish spots – the little stars that give the starling its name. Look closely and you will see a very glamorous bird, whereas the juvenile is a drab brown before it starts to get its stars, which appear patchily.

Adult starlings are ideal jizz case studies. They are unlike any other bird: they travel around in groups, descending like a wave of vultures to hustle and take over feeding stations. They strut everywhere, quite unlike the blackbirds and thrushes, which hop. And watch a starling as it stabs your lawn for leatherjackets; once the beak is in the ground, the birds lever it open before grabbing its favourite garden pest.

The television aerial is a favourite singing post for garden birds, and the starling will render its own version of birdsong from it: a mixture of wheezes, whistles, coughs and sneezes, often mimicking its more melodious neighbours, whilst all the time fluttering its short little wings. I remember one starling, in Dorset, that fooled me for some time with its perfect imitation of the eerie, lonely 'mew' of a buzzard.

Kingfishers

Starlings will generally be seen in flocks, whereas the other regular starling-sized birds will usually appear singly, like the most striking of all British birds and an occasional garden visitor, the blue, iridescent jewel, the kingfisher. Unmistakable, the kingfisher flies like a silver-blue bullet, all too often crashing headlong into patio doors and picture windows. It will also find a perch above the garden pond and spear fish, not for the koi carp (these are the province of the heron), but for fish small enough to fit in its oversized beak. It's true what they say: 'every bird or animal is a pest to somebody.'

Spotted woodpeckers

The other starling-sized bird that cannot help but catch the eye of any human is the greater spotted woodpecker, the bird you can hear 'rat-a-tat-tatting' in many woodlands. Unlike the sparrow-sized, lesser spotted woodpecker, the greater will visit bird feeding stations, and is particularly fond of peanuts and suet. Both woodpeckers have bold, black-and-white plumage with striking red caps, but neither of these spotted woodpeckers have any spots, so don't be fooled. It's rather like the black headed gull, an occasional visitor to front gardens, which has a chocolate-brown cap for some of the year, but a white one for the rest.

Blackbirds

Blackbirds are unmistakable, although only the cock bird is black. The female and juvenile blackbirds are brown, and one that I took in a few years ago was a definite yellowy-green colour, a rare colour mutation, although albino and partial albino blackbirds are comparatively common. If in doubt, look for the jizz and listen for the beautiful, fluted singing of the cock blackbird from the highest branch or television aerial, particularly at dawn or dusk. The blackbird is also responsible for the loud, clamouring alarm-call heard when a cat is about and the ear-shattering 'chink, chink' when it is mobbing a cat, owl or other predator.

Thrushes

The song thrush is far less bold than the blackbird, although it will vie for the best song, often choosing a very similar high perch to its cousin. And, just like the blackbird, it

The blackbird

Song thrush collecting worms for its young

will quarter the lawn looking for earthworms, often cocking its head to one side to get either a better view of its quarry or a sound to show it where to stab its beak. Nobody seems to be able to decide for sure the purpose of this head-cocking. Also, quite unlike the blackbird, which only sings during a few months of the year, a song thrush has been recorded offering its musical tones in every month, including early winter.

There are two larger thrushes that you may see in the garden in flocks during bad winters and these are likely to be the mistle thrushes and fieldfares, often accompanied by the smaller redwings. True, the mistle thrush is a resident and may also visit during the summer, but this fair-weather friend will be either alone or in a pair. The mistle thrush is just like a larger song thrush, but with much heavier chest markings. However, it is normally more wild than its small cousin and will not be seen quartering the lawn for earthworms or nesting in the trellis work. It will, in fact, nest high in the fork of a suitable tree and only then in very large gardens.

The fieldfare, however, will rarely nest in this country as it is only a winter visitor, along with the redwing, from its Scandinavian

A very bold bird, the mistle thrush

breeding grounds. Unmistakable as a thrush, it has the typical, heavily spotted chest of its mistle and song thrush cousins, but it has a markedly grey head and rump and a black tail.

Larger birds

There are not many garden birds larger than the mistle thrush or fieldfare, apart from those occasional piratical visitors, the magpies, jays, jackdaws and sparrowhawks, all of which are easily identified: the magpie is large with black-and-white plumage and a long tail; the jay is, once again, large, but with bright blue wing flashes and a typical bounding flight; the jackdaw is all black with a grey nape and blue eyes; and the sparrowhawk is a flash of brown as it snatches a small bird off the bird table or crashes into your patio door.

The other regular garden visitor is the collared dove. Smaller than a pigeon, but with similar seed-eating habits, its general plumage colour is an overall brown with a black collar, not to be confused with the much larger wood pigeon, which sports a white collar. Collared doves will often form a resident pair, who will come regularly to search for scraps and often become familiar favourites, especially when they bring their newly fledged offspring – one or two – to visit. If you feed your garden birds on the ground, then you may well attract a regular flock of collared doves, rather like those impossible flocks of feral pigeons that always seem to appear the moment food is put out.

Apart from the birds that I have mentioned there are, of course, many others that will visit gardens, especially those gardens which border woodland, moorland, coast or heath. Their identification will take many days of practise birdwatching, referring to bird manuals and listening to tapes of bird song. If you think that you may have a Cretzschmar's bunting or a penduline tit visiting your bird garden, then I would strongly recommend you buy one of the many bird identification books available and, in particular, I would recommend Collins' New Generation Guide – *Birds of Britain and Europe*, by Chris Perrins.

The sparrowhawk is usually just a blur of speed as it snatches a blue tit from the bird table

9 The Good, the Bad and the Ugly

I have lived for, fought for and often cried with, the devastated end of wildlife for many years and have, in that time, become firmly convinced that every wild bird, reptile, amphibian and mammal has its niche in the landscape, with its individual existence essential for the survival not just of its symbiotic hangers-on but also of its neighbours. There will be a similar natural order with the so-called lower creatures: the insects and other invertebrates, but that's when I sometimes let compassion and sentiment intervene and relieve a casualty of an excess of parasites or pathogens. I know that these little excursions into genocide have little effect on the overall picture, but for the moment my patient has a better chance of recovery and I know that nature will redress the balance.

However, with the more sophisticated orders of animals – the birds and mammals – an untimely and ill-conceived intervention, always by man, will cause a gross imbalance and often the demise of some species and the proliferation of others. For instance, the gamekeepers' obsession with swamping our countryside with pheasants has led to them almost wiping out most of the natural predators, like barn owls, buzzards, hawks and kites whose intervention kept the natural balance in the countryside. The unplanned spin-off is that now thousands of pheasants and other game birds raid the farmers' fields, and that there are plagues of rats previously curtailed by the avian hunters. And some of Britain's idiosyncratic farming practices do damage beyond the poisoning of the countryside. When wood pigeons – frequent and welcome visitors to many gardens, with their melodious and faithful love cooing – seem to be flocking in larger numbers, the landowners, already having accounted for the crows, magpies and squirrels which prey on pigeon nests, resort to blasting the wood pigeons out of the sky, completely destroying the natural balance so that more pigeons, crows and magpies and squirrels move into the now vacant territory. (Before man was on the scene the same crows, magpies and, then, red squirrels, kept the balance so that there was ample chance for all to exist side by side.)

A similar pattern is emerging in other areas, with million upon million of our garden birds being destroyed because of our blinkered obsession with one, non-indigenous species of predatory mammal.

Let me set the scene for you – a hen blackbird paired with that master songster, a cock blackbird, has a nest of scrawny youngsters secreted away in a thorn bush, hedge or even a garden climber. When the youngsters are fully feathered and on the verge of flying, the doting parents disperse them to various low-level hiding places in the vicinity. This proven system ensures that all the pair's eggs are not, literally, in one basket, but are in various animal's territories with the likelihood that some, and at least one of their progeny, will survive the attentions of the wild predators and reach maturity.

This has worked for many millions of years, with the natural balance dictating that if the predators were to take all of the chicks, all of the time, then they would eventually exterminate the bird species and they too would perish, this time from starvation. That is, unless man intervenes and supplements the predator's fast diminishing diet with readily available tins – cat food. There it is. The most devastating predator of all our garden birds, proved beyond any doubt, is I'm afraid to say the domestic cat.

Two scientists, Churcher and Lawton, recently conducted a survey into the habits of the domestic cat; their findings really astounded me. They found that each year in Britain 100 million small birds and other animals are killed by our domestic cats. The trouble is, like so many scientific papers, the revelations were lost on most of the cat owners of Britain and are probably now forgotten except by those, like me, caught in the front line of the battles between moggies and garden birds.

Churcher and Lawton only detailed those actually killed in the furore, yet I know from the thousands of 'catted' but living birds we take in at St Tiggywinkles that there are probably an equal number that only just escape with their lives. Add to these alarming totals the birds killed by the estimated one and a half million feral cats, and I believe we are looking at close on a quarter of a billion casualties every year. Admittedly, some of these casualties will be rats and mice, but the toll of hundreds of millions of lost birds, voles, lizards, frogs and others still hits home because, as usual, we are not doing enough to protect our wildlife. Even the next big killer, the motor car, 'only' accounts for two and a half million garden bird casualties – a mere fraction of the cats' depredations.

People knocking on our door with birds injured by cats – sometimes as often as six times a day if their cat has discovered a whole family of fledglings – often excuse the activities of the pet with a feeble, 'Well, it's only nature, after all!' I only wish it were, for nature would soon account for the excessive predation by restricting cat populations. But it's *not* nature.

The majority of cats are well fed and pampered by their human minders. Domestic cats do not have to compete with others for food, territory and breeding and are completely protected from adverse weather when the small bird, their prey, has to sit it out or scavenge a living in ice, snow or rain.

Moreover, the domestic cat has no natural place amongst the British fauna – it was probably bred from ancient Egyptian stock, natives of north Africa where larger relatives, the so-called big cats, would in their turn prey on their smaller cousins, keeping their population under control. When the unfortunate hen blackbird evolved in Britain, spending thousands of years working out a defence strategy, there was only the occasional wild cat (now known as the Scottish wild cat) preying predominantly on mammals and in their turn the wild cats were preyed on by the much larger lynx, now completely extinct in Britain. There was nowhere near the rapidly expanding seven and a half million domestic cats that she now has to contend with. She is quite incapable of doing so.

It's no good burying our heads in the sand: domestic cat predation on garden birds is a major ecological problem and has already started a decline in the numbers of our more familiar species – when did you last marvel at the full-throated song of the throstle, the song thrush, number two on the bird song-chart after the blackbird? They are disappearing rapidly; when a gamekeeper asks me about their demise and absence with concern, I know something is going drastically wrong.

We must do something about it. Of course, I am not suggesting we 'do away with cats!', but just asking that we be rational and careful. Five years ago, most pet owners had just one cat or two at the most. Now they have several, with some owning literally dozens. And they are all put outside at least once a day or at night. Having more than one cat usually results in another bevy of kittens to swell the numbers, causing even more adult cats to leave the overcrowded home to join the ever-increasing colonies of feral cats who, let's face it, are not really suited to a wild existence, judging by the pain they suffer from disease and starvation.

Thankfully, the Cat Action Trust has come to grips with the problems suffered by feral cat colonies. It saw that, uncontrolled, the numbers of unwanted cats swelling these colonies had earned them the insidious title 'vermin', giving the so-called pest controllers *carte blanche* to trap, poison and starve any that dared to rub shoulders with man. The Cat Action Trust has proved that a humane neutering policy keeps the colony's numbers to a healthy figure, stops unnecessary territorial

A very rare wryneck rescued from a cat

fighting (which still happens in multi-cat households) and leaves the cats to live a full, healthy and contented longer life.

But how can we bring some rationality to the out-of-hand domestic cat scene? We *can* keep the numbers down; we can certainly be less sentimental about cats and their predatory habits. You can help your own garden bird population by trying to make sure that your bird tables are of a cat-proof design. Put any nest boxes out of reach of the neighbourhood cats, and if necessary place loose wire netting both above and below any nest boxes and any nest that birds such as blackbirds, robins and thrushes will build in the most ludicrously accessible positions.

Unfortunately, the garden bird breeding season can stretch from March to September, so there is no way you can contain a cat for that length of time. Suffice it to say that if you do see a cat stalking something, even if it is invisible to you, or you see your cat about to raid a nest, then make a hell of a din and frighten it off time and again if necessary. I am not sure if the bucket-of-water repellent recommended by many commentators is classed as cruel or not, so I would suggest you resort to scaring the cat away from a distance . . .

Although it's true that cat-inflicted injuries make up the bulk of our work with garden birds, they cannot be held responsible for their misdemeanours. Man has put cats in this foreign environment and nobody can blame them for acting as their instincts demand. In fact, all but a very few of our casualties are the results of confrontations with man and the artificial environment he has created. In nature, most injurious encounters result in either the predator devouring its victim or disease making the sufferer vulnerable, usually resulting in death in the teeth or talons of another predator. The various parasite loads of wild birds do not, with the exception of a few specific species, generally interfere with the bird's life style. Once again, our old friend natural balance somehow informs the parasite to keep its numbers within bounds otherwise there would be a dead host, resulting in dead parasites.

However, nature doesn't get everything right. On occasions there are apparently mass natural deaths of wild birds soon after the arrival of exhausted migrants, both in spring, when birds arrive from southern climes, and in autumn, when fieldfares and redwings come in from Scandinavia. Once again, evolution has dictated migration as a pattern of bird behaviour, but nature doesn't always cater for the fact that its charges may arrive at their destination to find Britain devoid of the life-saving fuels – the insects, weed-seeds and wild fruit that could fill an empty stomach after an exhausting flight across the seas. Consequently many of the expected arrivals never make it. Once again, it is up to us to redress the balance.

Insecticides & Herbicides

Large numbers of insects, weeds and fruits have been exterminated by insecticides and their related herbicides, and it's these chemicals in the garden that are the silent killers of further millions of garden birds. It is not done by depriving our feathered visitors of a food source – we make sure they are fed by supplying bird tables and by carefully planting the right type of garden – but by the intoxicating, excruciating death through poisoning.

The number of those handsome birds, the woodpeckers, that I take in suffering from insecticidal poisoning often makes me wonder how any bird can survive in the countryside. And that is why our gardens are so important. The gardener need not be as gullible as the farmer, who often believes that routine spraying will enhance his cash crop. However there are still many gardeners who believe that insecticides and herbicides will make their roses brighter or will produce more runner beans for the Sunday lunch, oblivious to the chemical residues still held in those beans. When the sprayers finally realise that insects are responsible for helping turn their bean flowers into fruit (and that includes pollinating bees, ladybirds, moths and all butterflies), then perhaps they will discard their aerosols (safely) once and for all.

I feel very strongly about chemicals and the devastation they have caused to the environment. Even derris, which is supposed to be a safe insecticide, is particularly toxic to fish; can you guarantee that none is going to blow or be carried into your own or your neighbour's fish pond? At the hospital we only use, if we are forced to, one type of insecticide – pyrethrum powder – which is supposedly safe for all but insects. If you must use an insecticide, then please try only pyrethrum powder, but do remember that you are killing all insect species.

During most summers we will receive many whole nests of blue tit orphans where the parent birds are known to have died. We know from experience that the parents have died from eating poisoned insects and, horror upon horror, also know that these tiny babies have been fed poisoned insects – murdered by their unsuspecting parents. Gradually and inevitably the tiny balls of feathers start to die before our eyes. There is nothing anybody can do about it – there are no such things as antidotes to most man-made poisons.

It's up to us gardeners to put away our potions, powders and spray cans and then sit back and marvel at how a nesting song thrush, if there are two left, can account for 10,000 caterpillars, flies, grubs and snails for every brood of healthy youngsters. (And please note here that snails can carry residues of slug pellets in their tissues – pellets that, to my mind, seem to be more adept at killing hedgehogs and thrushes than they are at stopping gastropods.) See how each one of a visiting, bustling mob of starlings can probe your lawn and catch fifty leatherjackets in fifteen

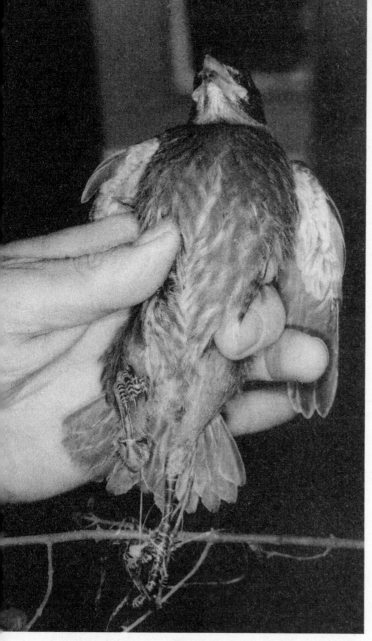

The perils of cotton. The bird was found hanging by its feet, tangled in cotton used over fruit crops

minutes, as well as aerating the top surface for you. These are just two of the benefits of a chemical-free garden and everything, including the land itself, is safe and clean.

Other hazards

Unfortunately, all around the garden there are hazards that the average garden bird seems to seek out. In our quest for unblemished garden flowers and produce we do seem, albeit inadvertently, to set traps for many small birds who might be innocently raiding our raspberry crop or pecking the petals off our prize chrysanthemums. Believe me, the death from a cat's claw or the sting of insecticide is nothing compared to the slow, garrotte of black cotton strung across seed beds. Sometimes the birds die, sometimes they are rescued, but many escape with cotton still attached – painful ligatures that slowly cut into the flesh, severing circulation until toes, feet and even legs drop off, leaving the birds unable to perch. They finally collapse, exhausted, never to recover.

If only we, as consumers, did not worry about eating fruit that has been pecked by birds. Or if there is a worry, why don't we plant more than we need, so that there is enough for everyone: people, birds, voles, moths, the whole lot? And if you *must* cover your garden produce, use safe, rigid netting like that marketed by Netlon. This will be safe for hedgehogs as they cannot get tangled and you will find that birds can land safely, be thwarted in their quest for your fruit, but can still fly away unscathed.

There are alternatives to extra planting or netting, in the form of scarecrows and bird scarers, but they do become familiar to your local birds, requiring you to set your mind constantly to new ideas: a small portable radio blasting out pop music is said to be effective, but hardly conducive to the peace and sanctuary we expect from our gardens. And to have a commercial scarer that went 'bang!' every five minutes would create havoc with your neighbourhood *entente cordiale*. Silver foil bows threaded on to lengths of thick wire can be effective for a time. The use of string should be resisted as this soon frays and, once again, will trap the birds once they are familiar with your deterrent and start using it as a jumping-off perch on to your seedbed.

Silhouette cutouts of cats, owls or hawks, especially if they have sparkling eyes added with the help of Christmas glitter spray, will keep off the more timid birds. I have a very antiquated, carved, wooden hawk-shape that was made as a bird scarer. Unfortunately, I will never find out if it works as I want to encourage birds into my garden, even if I have to plant extra peas and raspberries.

But, whatever you do, please resist those chemical bird repellents. Whenever any extra chemical, no matter how innocuous it seems, is introduced to the garden, it will create an upheaval at some level of the natural balance, encouraging you to buy another chemical to redress that error – and so on. A great marketing ploy to encourage the sales of even more types of chemical.

While I do not generally advocate the use of bird scarers, there is one situation where an efficient one is absolutely essential. This is by the new-style picture windows that are so attractive to householders but are usually invisible to fast-flying birds, especially when they can see a potential flight path through to another picture window on the other side of the house. Without curtains, the 'through lounge' concept is inviting yet deadly to many birds, who collide with the windows. It results in, at best, concussion, but more often than not in brain damage and instant death.

Apart from leaving your windows dirty there seem to be very few effective deterrents available; even curtains create a reflection, offering a flight path. Once again, silhouette cutouts of cats, owls, sparrowhawks and even people are said to be effective, but I often wonder what a whizzing sparrowhawk thinks of another perched in its territory. Might it actually attack your deterrent at that familiar sparrowhawk breakneck speed? The Swiss are quite convinced of its effectiveness and often have sparrowhawk effigies actually engraved into the glass.

A researcher at Muhlenberg College, Pennsylvania, Daniel Klem, Jr, estimates that between 98 and 976 million birds are killed annually in window collisions in the USA.

Contrary to established belief, the birds do not usually die of broken necks but of brain haemorrhages. To reduce the incidence of collisions he suggests that bird tables and baths should be placed either less than 30 centimetres from the window, or at a far greater distance, possibly over 20 metres away. Collision with windows is apparently more damaging to bird populations than we in Britain had imagined. There is one solution, which is to slope the windows to reflect the ground below them. Obviously it would be an impossible task to replace existing windows all over the country, but perhaps architects could take note and incorporate bird safety design in new projects.

I only wish that there were an easy solution as I would dearly love to find an effective deterrent to stop the regular flow of concussed or dying birds brought to the hospital. If anybody has a solution, they could write to me at St Tiggywinkles and perhaps someone could run another public-awareness campaign to stop the slaughter.

Having cardboard effigies of hawks, cats and owls amongst the furry dice and Garfields in the windows of cars would, unfortunately, have little effect in reducing the casualties from the other major hazard to garden birds – road traffic accidents, or RTAs, as they are abbreviated to on our Hospital admittance cards. In fact, more junk in the windows would probably increase the incidence of serious road accidents because of the further impaired visibility.

Every year, when spring is in the air, the whole blackbird population seems to go love-crazy, whizzing backwards and forwards across highways and byways at a suicidal 30 centimetres above the road. I am sorry to say that it is nigh on impossible to miss them, nearly as impossible as missing the stragglers of a gang of sparrows or the flocks of finches that bob and weave into your vision at the last moment. Many concerned people have wracked their brains for a solution but, so far, have all come to the conclusion that there is no safe way to avoid the inevitable.

Distressed drivers, men and women, turn up at the hospital in tears because they have hit one of these blackbirds, sparrows or finches. I try to reassure them that there is often no way of avoiding the accident apart from braking safely. Even swerving may not miss the bird and will more than likely result in a collision with oncoming traffic. All you can do is gather up any birds that survive the impact, keep them warm and get them to a wildlife rescue facility where corticosteroids, fluid therapy and antibiotics can often save a bird's life.

Predators

Birds who encounter a natural hazard rarely survive. The hazard is often in the form of one of the main predators on garden birds, on the lookout for an easy meal. And therein lies the crux of the matter – a meal. We are usually

A picture-window collision case, a kingfisher, flies back to freedom

spectators to the cut and thrust of a natural predator's visit and can do little to prevent it. In fact, should we intervene? Personally, I would, but only to deter the predator if I was quick enough. I would never harm it, whether it be a quicksilver sparrowhawk or a much maligned magpie. These birds are trying to eke a living by the only means they know. It's not easy being a predator – most meals evade capture and if you kill and eat too much the larder will be bare for the next meal.

For some reason many people see the magpie as a villain because it carefully stalks its prey, often by sitting and watching the comings and goings of parent birds to their eggs or nestlings. Sounds a bit familiar, doesn't it? Not unlike the *modus operandi* of our friend the cat. There has been much talk about the supposed glut of magpies over the last few years. True, everywhere you look there seem to be gangs of magpies exploiting the weak, unprotected, unwary and dead. But then surely this is only evolution seeking out the weak links, the carelessly positioned nest or the badly hidden youngster? Nature wants only the cleverest blackbird or the most wary thrush to breed, forever passing on their finer points to their offspring.

I don't worry about the apparent glut of magpies. For one thing, it's a bird that is difficult to overlook, with its bold black, white and green plumage and cackling conversation. I bet that a flock of owls in the same field, if ever such a thing occurred, would go unnoticed by ninety-nine per cent of the population. Most wild species have dramatic rises and falls in populations, hence the well-known but poorly understood apparent mass suicide of lemmings when their numbers exceed the food available. That occasional night-time visitor to gardens, the tawny owl, will breed prolifically when its prey, voles and fieldmice, have had a good breeding season.

Unless tin lids are removed completely, birds and mammals can easily become trapped

Magpie numbers will drop, especially if they over-exploit their food source – but there's the rub: garden bird numbers may be down but the magpie has, like the fox and the gull, learned to profit from man's excessive waste and is not now wholly reliant on natural food resources. Hopefully its attention is also been drawn to that new food source, giving the smaller birds a chance to recover. You see, every time there is a problem with Britain's wildlife then man, often inadvertently, is having some effect.

Killing magpies is not an answer, because when one of the larger species is put under unnatural pressure or a vacuum created, then nature decrees, somehow, that the victim species breed more prolifically. For instance, foxes breed more regularly in areas where they are persecuted and often fail to breed when there is a stable population. It makes no difference how many magpies are killed; by the end of the breeding season their numbers are replenished. And why kill them? Only a gamekeeper, would dream of killing a sparrowhawk for plucking a blue tit off the bird table or condemning a great spotted woodpecker for breaking into a nest box and taking the young birds or eggs. Magpies are doing what comes naturally and, hopefully, in spite of man's intervention with waste as food, nature will take its toll and numbers moderate themselves.

The very close cousin of the magpie, another crow, the jay, may also be a visitor to the garden. However, its swooping visits to steal peanuts off the bird table or acorns from under the oak tree never seem to have the deliberate mischief of the magpies and I doubt, even though they are predatory, that they would give any cause for concern about their intentions towards nesting garden birds. Mind you, there are always going to be exceptions, so never become complacent that this glamorous bird is your regular visitor.

It's *worth* taking a few precautions, such as placing bird tables well out in the open and not moving foliage to look at nests (which leaves a signal for the raiders). Drilled metal plates can be bought or made to protect nest boxes from squirrels and woodpeckers and a reversed cone fixed in front of the hole will keep out weasels (who are very fond of a brood of young birds or even the eggs). That's nature again, but perhaps it's our prerogative as compassionate human beings to intervene mildly – far better than resorting to killing as an attempt at a solution.

At the other end of the spectrum, there are some situations where the garden bird can become the intruder and then man has to intervene, if only to protect the birds from other humans. Wild birds are lucky in that they have powerful support and in the main are protected by law no matter how plentiful they are (unlike mammals only a very few of which enjoy protection). It is an offence to kill, injure or take any wild bird, its nest, or eggs, or to have in possession (injured birds excepted, see Chapter 10) any wild bird, egg or part thereof. In essence, this means that wild birds are completely protected. So think twice before knocking those house martin nests down in order to decorate the house, and don't trap swift nests when relining a roof, as one householder in Tring did – to twenty nests in her roof. We did manage to rescue most of the swiftlets and foster them into other swift nests elsewhere.

The fine for each offence can be £400, with some fines reaching £2,000 for each bird, nest or egg. There are a few exceptions where some landowners are permitted to interfere with nests and eggs, but I am not going to list these. To me, it's good that all birds can be protected and people are no longer tempted to rear baby birds as cage birds or resort to traps or poisons to protect their fruit crops.

Owners of large fruit and vegetable farms are the main protagonists in the fight with small birds. However, the amount of damage actually incurred is small and should be evaluated against the cost of control methods. On an enormous scale, a research project carried out at East Malling Research Station in Kent actually proved that even though 1,000 plum trees were attacked by sparrows, less than ten per cent were severely damaged. Another interesting survey in Kent revealed that orchards sited away from woodland are not attacked by bullfinches, the supposed arch-enemy of all fruit farmers.

Unfortunately, the same innocence cannot be claimed for the latest bird man has introduced into Britain – the ring-necked parakeet. Their success in the south-east of England should now be a vivid reminder of the perils of introducing completely alien species. The ring neck, originally from West Africa and the Middle East, is now firmly entrenched in the Home Counties. You would think that it could not survive through our occasional bad winters but it does – relying mainly on food put out on bird tables, with flocks of up to twenty descending colourfully into gardens as far west as Sunbury-on-Thames. The ring neck is a strong, confident bird, which soon bullies other species out of its way and thinks it only normal to pirate nest holes of starlings and woodpeckers, even if the residents are brooding eggs or youngsters.

If this isn't enough to get them a bad name, then the damage they do to orchards puts them high on the fruit grower's hate list. Unlike most fruit-eating birds, which will concentrate on one fruit until it has been eaten, the ring neck usually takes just one bite out of each apple or plum, leaving dozens of the fruit permanently scarred and open to disease. And because they are in an alien environment, there is really no predator that has evolved to keep them under control; except, perhaps, for the occasional weasel which may raid a nest, or an extra large sparrowhawk who may taste success with a young bird. I think that over the next few years we

Starlings meet their first ring-necked parakeet

shall see an increase in the population of ring necks further west and possibly north into the Midlands. They are a bright splash of colour and interest on the bird table but, perhaps, because of the damage they wreak on local bird populations, we should not encourage them into our gardens if we can avoid it.

We have seen since the 1950s the phenomenal spread of the collared dove into gardens and fields. Unlike the ring-necked parakeet this introduction, though unexplained, has been entirely natural, rather like the decline of the barn owl, which is unexplained when the tawny and little owls are doing so well.

Other incursions by garden birds into our lives are no real nuisance, although the incessant, monotonous chirping of a house sparrow outside the early morning bedroom window can drive many to the border of intolerance. Some small birds, mostly tits, have the other, at times infuriating habit of pecking away the putty around windows or, even more annoying, of entering the house and tearing off strips of wallpaper. Nobody knows why they do it, although it has been mooted that they are tempted by the linseed oil in putty, with the wallpaper tearing resembling tearing thin bark off trees to reach insects hiding underneath.

I often hear complaints about the droppings that collect under house martin nests and I quickly recommend a simple shelf under each one, or a daily hosing of the ground, to keep the problem under control. Many people without house martins nesting under their eaves would love to have the problem. But even with artificial nest sites created you are still going to be very lucky to persuade any house martins to desert a site that has been in their family for generations.

Birds nesting in or around houses are the subject of resentment by many householders.

With not only their noise and mess but the possibility of a massive parasite influx, they can create a great deal of hostility, particularly if the birds happen to be sparrows or starlings. In fact, birds have a very controlled range of ectoparasites and very rarely harbour fleas, which are the great worry of many people. And, as with hedgehogs, birds' parasites are entirely host-specific, with no bird flea or louse ever dreaming of leaving its host. What is more, like all parasites, they tend to live symbiotically with their hosts, only very rarely getting out of control and debilitating their hosts so much that they can easily be caught for hospital treatment.

10 A Bird in the Hand

Picking up an injured bird

The easier it is to catch a bird, the greater must be its plight. It's not your ability to catch or how you go about catching it, but very simply the fact that if you can catch a wild bird then something is wrong with it. If in doubt about any bird, see how near you can get to it. Every bird has a built-in flee response which triggers when you approach. If it makes no attempt to flee, then the bird is in serious trouble and can easily be picked up. With a small bird, just hold it one handed across the shoulders, making sure to keep the wings closed to the body. In fact, this is good advice when handling any bird, using either one hand or both for larger birds such as pigeons and crows.

None of the smaller birds – pigeons and smaller – can do you any harm, though some will bite you, especially sparrows. Your feeling of confidence in handling a bird will make your job easier and keep the bird quieter. Some species, notably blackbirds and thrushes, will cry out as you pick them up; do

not let their cries shock you into relaxing your grip or else you will have to catch the bird all over again.

Simple first aid

When the bird is in your hand, cover its head with a small towel. This will keep it quiet until you can find a cardboard box to put it in. Never put a wild bird into a bird cage at this stage, as it will panic and do itself considerable harm in trying to escape. Remember, it thinks you are going to eat it, not help it.

Put the box on a radiator or line it with a hot water bottle covered with a towel. Warmth will help the bird settle and start the process of coping with the shock of first the trauma and then the capture. It's always a good idea to put an old towel in the bottom of the box to give the bird something on which to grip. Never put hay or straw in with an injured bird as it may lead to respiratory problems.

If you are picking up larger birds like crows, owls or hawks, then there is some

First Aid for Injured Wild Birds

Place the casualty in a warm, dark container on an old towel (not hay or straw). Do not offer any liquid.

After 2 hours check the casualty, its condition and the extent of its injuries.

If it is still unconscious or if there are any obvious fractures or dislocations, it should be referred to a sympathetic vet or reputable bird rescue centre, unless you feel expert enough to give help yourself, see Chapter 11.

If the bird seems fully recovered, let it fly around an enclosed room and then release it where it was found.

At all times keep the bird warm and quiet and do not offer any liquid.

danger to you from their beaks and talons. A crow, rook, magpie, jackdaw or jay have quite a painful bite, but an elastic band wrapped around the tip of the beak stops any problems. Crows will also grab you with their feet. It will not do any harm but it will hurt. It's different with owls and hawks – their talons will puncture the skin so be very careful to control both legs as well as wings. The bird may or may not bite; once again it is not dangerous but may be quite painful and bites are to be avoided if at all possible.

These are birds that have been found lying stationary or comatose. However, many casualties have the ability to flee and when

moving are very difficult to grab using just your hands. A large net is ideal and I always recommend that people borrow a landing net from an angler; small nets can cause damage to the bird. Failing this, an old blanket or coat can be thrown over the fugitive with the added darkness often calming the bird before it is picked up.

If a bird can fly, then you will probably not be able to catch it, but if it has obviously got a problem then it really is worth trying.

Before you make your attempt at any capture, always look around and try to spot any cover and escape routes. Your bird, if it can move, will move away from you, so make sure that it does not flee into a road or your garden pond. Try to drive it into a cul-de-sac or even the house or a garden shed. Once confined, it will be much easier to catch.

Once your bird is safely inside a warm cardboard box . . . don't do anything. Do not lift the lid to see if it's all right; it will probably dive for the gap, forcing you to catch it again. Do not try to feed it or give it anything to drink, just leave it alone to settle, then check it after about an hour. If it has recovered and shows no signs of damage to its wings, legs, head or body, then leave it in the box and release it the following morning.

Should it need more help than this, there are some simple procedures that will work. For many years, and I still hear it, people have said to me that they had taken in injured birds, often on more than one occasion, and that those birds always died. They probably did and would still die, except that wildlife rescue centres have slowly evolved techniques to save injured birds. There are no short cuts – if you want to save an injured bird then either go quickly to a wildlife rescue centre, or else learn some of the simple first aid techniques that have proved essential to saving a bird's life.

The incident of the starlings and pigeons caught in the explosion at Pitstone proved to be a graphic example of basic capture techniques, using landing nets and a few basic procedures to combat their initial trauma.

In fact, once the first batch of pigeons and starlings were settled in at the hospital, after receiving first aid, we prepared to go back to Pitstone to see if the fire brigade would allow us access to the explosion site in order to rescue any more survivors. The extra volunteers were to stay at the hospital to organise extra medical supplies and prepare warm cages for the expected influx. The initial treatment of eyes and injections would take place in the 'surgery', then the birds would be carried to the intensive care section in the garage, where they would be given fluids and sorted into suitable cages.

As most wild bird casualties require only the minimum of treatment, we knew from experience that the medicines we would need would only be: long-acting amoxycillin, which is an injectable antibiotic; dexametha-

It is a wonder this great tit had survived so long in the wild before coming to the hospital for a beak trim

sone, a corticosteroid; a soothing eye ointment with antibiotic in it and Lectade, a rehydrating fluid to be given by mouth. With these four items anybody can deal with practically any wild bird casualty, but as we did not know how many casualties to expect we had to set about collecting dozens of tubes of chloramphenicol eye ointment, bottles of antibiotics and corticosteroids, gallons of Lectade and roll after roll of kitchen towel; all to be ready on standby when the rescue team returned from the cement works, we could not know when.

Basic First-Aid Kit

- Cardboard box
- Towel
- Hot water bottle
- Kitchen roll
- Fairy Liquid washing-up liquid
- Tweezers
- Scissors
- Small torch
- Cotton wool
- Cotton buds
- Savlon – for bathing wounds
- Swarfega liquid cleanser (for tarred feathers)
- Dermisol Multi-cleanse solution
- Forceps and artery forceps
- Spreull's needles, 2, 5 & 10 ml syringes
- 19g sterile needle (to lance abcesses and subcutaneous emphysema)
- Bamboo for cutting up to make splints
- Lightweight leather gloves (for handling hedgehogs and birds of prey)
- Elastic bands for restraining corvid beaks
- Zinc oxide plaster tape (1cm)
- Chloramphenicol eye ointment
- Beechams Lectade
- International Rehydrating Fluid (see p. 149)

Sue had kept in constant contact with the fire control office and, at last, in the early evening, we were given the necessary clearance to return to the site.

Once again Colin, Nigel, Andy and I donned our winter togs and headed back to the devastated scene. It was dark and eerie as the steam hissed invisibly from the giant pipe and puny spotlights picked out parts of the works complex. The snow had melted, leaving a small, icy cold lake of slush and water between us and the wrecked building. We waded into the blackness, saving our torches for inside. The white-helmeted fire fighter came to meet us, warning us of the dangers and leading us to the top of a metal gantry that fell away into the blackness that was the scene of the explosion. The cement company insisted on no photographs, but somebody had to know how these birds had suffered, so I had my camera under my coat, while Colin had his Christmas present miniature in his pocket.

Gingerly, in the yellow light of our torches, we almost felt our way down and further down, expecting at any time to feel solid ground. It was a long time coming and then when it did, it proved to be an obstacle course of black and charred bodies. Then Nigel shouted, 'There's a live one,' as a tiny, battered starling scampered out of the torch beam. Andy spotted another, and then there was a pigeon disturbed as Colin dived into a particularly dark corner to grab three starlings at once. Soon we were all running around, cramming dozens of birds into our boxes. None of them could fly as their feathers had melted to stumps in the explosion, but boy could they run!

We were soon covered from head to foot in dirt and soot, and I was glad I had insisted that we all wore surgical gloves, or else our hands would have surely suffered, especially as we grabbed birds trapped in hot ashes and cooled them in puddles – the only water available.

For hour after hour we groped around the ruined building, filling box after box with helpless birds. Eventually we ran out of boxes so had to search the rest of the works, commandeering any receptacle we could find that would hold birds.

With the ground floor well quartered and most of the birds rescued, we felt we had to look to the gantries stretching away above us into another black abyss. There had to be injured birds up there, as every so often a frantically flapping starling had come plummeting down as we worked below, to land with a plop in one of the puddles around our feet.

Andy and I had always worked as a team on rescues so delegated ourselves to make the perilous ascent. By then we only had one working torch between us and I carried the box as Andy highlighted the footway up into the roof. Every ledge or landing held little bundles of shivering feathers too frightened to

move in the darkness, standing rigid next to their dead brothers and sisters. Thankfully, they were mostly receptive to being picked up, although the occasional one would scurry over the edge into the blackness below. About halfway up I bent to pick up one casualty, only to realise that he had died standing up, head up, resigned to his fate.

Our box was beginning to fill up. It's surprising how heavy starlings can be, and I was worried that the bottom would fall out, scattering our charges all over the floor below. Andy volunteered to go down and change boxes, but had to take our fast-fading torch, leaving me perched on a plank, unable to move in the total darkness. It seemed like forever before he returned, but we were soon pressing on upwards, collecting more and more bedraggled birds.

At the top of the gantry, directly above the remains of the silo, there were starlings tucked into every inaccessible place, giving us many heart-stopping moments as we stretched to reach their little ledges. Eventually we decided that we had all the live ones we were going to find that night and almost crawled in the now dim yellow torchlight, back down to terra firma.

Our two Toyota estates were jam-packed full of boxes, nets, dirty clothing and untold amounts of soot, slush and grime, ready for the trip back to the hospital. Our small team was waiting: we had phoned ahead, and so after some welcome hot tea and crumpets it was down to work on our production line, even though it was nearly midnight. However, the exercise in treating all those starlings and pigeons proved to be a vivid illustration of how to cope with a typical garden bird casualty, although we did have hundreds to deal with.

Life-saving antibiotics

Our first line of attack was to give each bird an injection of antibiotics and corticosteroids to counter shock and the inevitable lung damage caused by the explosion and fireball. Margaret Mortham, a phlebotomist and our 'legalised vampire', who in fact runs our office, teamed up with Andy as they were both experienced not only in giving injections to birds but, just as important, in handling and safely disposing of hypodermic needles.

Our antibiotic of choice with birds is long-acting amoxycillin, administered daily, whereas in mammals it is given every other day. This is because a bird's metabolism is far more active than a mammal's, utilising the antibiotics at a faster rate. The procedure is to inject it sub-cutaneously, just under the skin to the right side of the bird's breastbone.

With the bird temporarily held on its back you can easily feel the breastbone and, with garden birds, can gently part the feathers to expose the skin. Then the needle – I recommend a 25g orange or 23g blue – can be simply slid just under the skin, and the right amount of antibiotic – 250mg/kg of long-acting amoxycillin – can be injected.

People may say that this really is a job for a veterinary surgeon, but my experience has been that if you discuss the situation with your local vet he may well allow you the antibiotics to carry out the medication yourself and will even show you how to do it. At the moment there is a bit of a quandary in the veterinary world, with the British Veterinary Association and its allied British Small Animal Veterinary Association, recommending that member vets carry out work on small wild animals and birds totally free, provided it is within working hours. My experience has been that many vets will not even look at a wild animal or bird and also that the majority of wild casualties occur at the most inopportune hours, certainly not between nine and five, and certainly not on a weekday.

Because of this apparent lack of veterinary interest in wild bird casualties, I am sure many practices would be more than willing to assist anybody else taking in and caring for wildlife and helping with the pressures of prescription-only medicines, to prevent their practices being overrun with free patients.

If you come across many bird casualties, particularly those damaged by cats, then it is probably impractical to keep running to the vet and you will probably soon use up any goodwill you have generated. I mention cats again, at this juncture, because we have found that one simple injection of long-acting amoxycillin, administered as I have described, is the only way to save some birds caught by our feline friends. I know that, by rights, a course of antibiotics should always be completed, but in extensive trials with catted birds we have found that the catching up and handling of birds for repeat injections did more harm, stressing the birds and often killing them.

I know this all sounds very technical and beyond the realms of the casual gardener, but without just the basic one injection your bird casualty will die. If you are worried about handling needles and injecting birds and there is not a wildlife centre near you, then I am afraid that you will have to pay a visit to your vet, just for that one, life-saving injection.

Let me explain why the one-off injection has proved to be such a life-saver. For many years it was accepted that a bird caught by a cat would die within forty-eight hours. In fact, this inevitability was called 'forty-eight-hour syndrome' and was put down to irreversible shock. However, recent research in America has shown that the birds usually succumbed to a septicaemia, more commonly known as blood-poisoning, brought on by the bacteria *Pasteurella multicoda*, present on a cat's teeth, and that death could occur anything up to two weeks after the cat attack.

The change in our success rate since we have been using the one-off injection has been phenomenal. We now get very upset if we lose a catted bird which is not too badly injured. In fact, there may be no apparent injury, but the bird must have its injection regardless.

I mentioned that we only give one antibiotic injection to avoid handling, and this really is absolutely crucial, although some birds will still die of a heart attack just at the touch of a hand. If you see your casualty start to reach and gasp for breath with its beak open, immediately cover it with a towel or put it back into its warm dark box until it recovers its composure. To keep on holding the bird will bring about its death in literally seconds.

Once the catted bird, or any injured bird for that matter, has received its first aid, if you like, then put it into a warm cage with other birds of a similar size. I do not know why, but a bird caged on its own seems to die, but one thrust into the hurly-burly of a communal cage seems to thrive on the adrenalin competition produces. (Just a little footnote to this – song thrushes may be the same size as blackbirds, but will survive much better if put in with the smaller sparrows, robins and finches.)

Side effects of injuries

A common side effect of a cat attack that worries many people, is the sudden appearance on various parts of the bird of enormous balloon-like swellings. They may even occur around the legs, preventing the bird from standing, or on the neck, making it impossible for the bird to keep its head up straight. Take a closer look and you will see that these swellings are transparent. They are in fact subcutaneous emphysema, caused by a damaged air sac, part of a bird's respiratory system. To disperse them, simply 'pop' them like you would a balloon, but using a sterile hypodermic needle. They may inflate again but will eventually stay down as the leak in the air sac closes.

The starlings in our explosion exercise also received an initial injection of the corticosteroid, dexamethasone, as well as the antibiotics. Dexamethasone should always be accompanied by an injection of antibiotics and is ideal for countering not only stress and lung distress but is instrumental in relieving cerebral pressure, especially after collision accidents. It is effective also in expanding and encouraging the circulatory system, which is compromised in stress incidents, but please never treat it as a 'cure all', as its side effect is to suppress the body's own immune system, hence the complimentary antibiotic injection. Always be very wary of using a corticosteroid if there is infection or bleeding.

We were using 'dex' in the starlings to improve their respiratory chances and to counter some of the stress, but in the garden bird world it always seems to be needed for concussive injuries.

Concussion

Picture the scene: you are sitting watching an afternoon television programme when, thump, something hits your picture window, conjuring up images of neighbourhood hooligans. You rush out on to your patio to find your hooligan, feathers ruffled, lying inert and tiny on the path, feet in the air. Another casualty of the picture window, who hopefully will be fit for release after a couple of hours' recovery in a dark, warm cardboard box. There may be longer-term damage but, provided the patient can stand and fly and its head is held straight, it can and should be released. If, after two hours, it still appears dazed or is holding its head at a peculiar angle, or even upside down, then there is a more severe concussion or even brain damage and this is where an injection of dexamethasone, with its complimentary antibiotics, by your vet, may help the casualty make a more speedy recovery.

Although not truly garden birds, there are two spectacular fliers who are always flying into picture windows and ending up unconscious on some patio or other. These two, the iridescent kingfisher and wild sparrowhawk, both fly at incredible speeds and when they hit, they hit, often completely knocking themselves out for some time. Both are wholly protected by Schedule Four of the Wildlife and Countryside Act of 1981, so if you should find one injured in your garden, it must be handed over to a Licensed Rehabilitation Keeper, whose name will be on a list kept by the Department of the Environment at Bristol. Never, ever, try to give a concussed bird anything to drink and be sure to wear gloves or cover its talons when handling a

A kestrel after an accident

A bird in the house

If a bird flies in through an open window, it will panic, and you should keep calm and do the following: do not immediately try to catch it, but turn out any lights, close the doors and pull all the curtains except those over the window where it came in. It should, if chased, make for that one exit.

The other bird intruders usually come down the chimney. Luckily, if you have an open fireplace, you should be able to steer the bird, usually a starling, jackdaw or owl, towards a window exit, then clean up the soot it leaves behind. If you have a fitted gas fire then usually the local gas board, who I believe have an arrangement with the R S P C A, will call and release the bird. Both these types of incident occur frequently – surely a good reason for having bird-proof cowls fitted to your chimneys and flues.

If your starling, jackdaw or owl had fallen down the chimney onto an open fire, then you would have to treat it just as we were treating the pigeons and starlings burnt at Pitstone, with particular attention being given to the eyes that are so crucial to any bird.

Eye injuries

All the eyes of our Pitstone casualties had been seared closed in the heat of the fireball and needed intricate and careful treatment on the next stage of our production line.

Sharon and Nigel Brock, our next-door neighbours, took charge of the eye clinic.

sparrowhawk; or, for that matter, any bird of prey.

However, unlike the catted bird, many concussed birds will recover without injectable medications. If dexamethasone and antibiotics are not available, then a warm, dark box may well see your bird casualty recovered enough after a couple of hours to be released back into the garden. I would, however, recommend releasing kingfishers near a suitable stream and sparrowhawks on the edge of a deciduous wood.

A typical blackbird road-traffic casualty – 'Noble' the blackbird before treatment for a damaged eye

With his eye fully recovered, 'Noble' is ready for release

Many garden birds, especially collared doves, attract eye problems and in most cases the method of treatment is exactly the same as Sharon and Nigel carried out on the starlings. It is a procedure anyone can carry out.

It's usually very helpful to strap the bird completely in an old towel, leaving just the head exposed. This keeps the bird reasonably calm and controls the wings and legs, enabling you to concentrate on the job at hand.

First off, with a cotton bud moistened in warm, salt water (one teaspoon of salt to a pint of water) the sealed lids are gently moistened, wiping off any exudate until the lids can be carefully pulled open. Then the eye itself is flushed with a syringe of the warm salt solution and a mild antibiotic ointment, chloramphenicol, is applied, making sure it lubricates under both lids and the so-called 'third eyelid', the nitating membrane. I would not recommend the use of any other eye ointment, especially those containing corticosteroids, as they may aggravate any wound or infection you may not have noticed. Ideally, the chloramphenicol ointment should be applied several times each day.

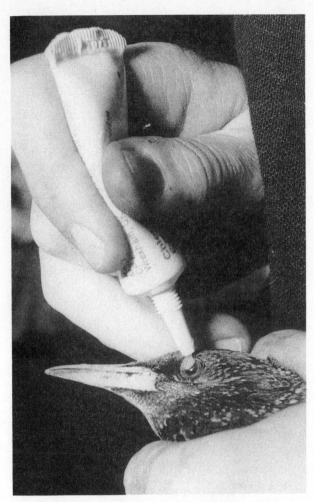

Each bird had soothing ointment applied to each eye

Eyes have a remarkable power of recovery and even damaged eyes will recover after bathing in salt water and treating with chloramphenicol ointment, known as 'coo' for short.

Damaged feathers

Also, any bird that has been damaged in a fire will have some feather trauma. Our birds all had various degrees of damage where the explosion had burnt away or melted their primary and secondary feathers.

Many people do not understand how a feather works but it is important, particularly with the ace fliers – the swifts, swallows and birds of prey – to know whether a feather is going to grow again or whether it will remain a hindrance until the next moult.

We all know what a feather looks like but take a closer look and see how it is made up of a main stem with branches coming off at regular intervals, all locked together with tiny barbules that keep the plumage water and weatherproof while still providing the lift needed for flying. When a feather first grows in a young bird or during the moult, it is covered by a thin sheath to protect the growing feather; at this stage it is fuelled by a copious blood supply. In fact, if the feather is broken or cut now it will bleed profusely, often giving the finder of an injured bird fears of a fatal haemorrhage. But, like any bleeding, it can be easily stopped with a pressure pad or by clamping with artery forceps.

Any broken feather will stay broken until the next moult, when it will drop out and be replaced by a new one. The feather itself will not regrow. This is not a major problem for a blackbird or a sparrow, but for a swift or a sparrowhawk just one feather out of place could mean serious trouble. If the feather is just bent but is generally intact, then sometimes it can be straightened by steaming over a boiling kettle. There is a system for larger birds, especially birds of prey, called 'imping', where a portion of a feather similar to the broken one can be glued to the stump as a stop-gap measure. This is impractical with small birds and possibly the only solution, drastic though it is, is to pluck the broken feather. Only then will a new one grow through.

Plucking may sound drastic and, in my opinion, should only be resorted to if you are seriously concerned about a bird's flying ability. Mind you, if a patient has any sort of wound then it is absolutely essential to pluck the feathers around the site to prevent the feathers falling in and contaminating it.

Cleaning contaminated feathers

The feathers are essential for the wellbeing of any bird and, rather like the scales of a fish, will not do their job if they are damaged or contaminated in any way. Only ever handle a bird with washed hands and *never* apply any grease or lanolin to a bird's plumage. Needless to say, also always wash your hands after handling a bird. Garden birds are always getting contaminated in some way or another. I suppose it's inevitable, living in such close proximity to man and his untidy habits. I have taken in small birds covered in paint, paint stripper, 'doggie-loo' chemicals, tar,

cement and, of course, I have taken in birds which have fallen in that tray of oil left over from when you last serviced the car. You have to take each mess as it comes, but in each case you must take care that your cleaner does not inflict more damage than the contaminant already has.

For instance, although white spirit or turpentine will clean off paint and tar, it

All sorts of bird fall into open oil cans and trays in garages. This is a little owl

will probably also kill the bird. A safe hand-cleanser like Swarfega will take longer to work but will be much kinder to the bird. However, do not use Swarfega on an oiled bird. There has been extensive research done by the University of Newcastle upon Tyne into the most effective way of cleaning oiled sea birds without impairing their waterproofing system. Although waterproofing and weatherproofing are not quite so important for a garden bird, a small bird is easily chilled if it gets wet, so we owe it to them to use the best method possible in order to get them released as soon as we can.

There are, once again, many misunderstandings about a bird's waterproofing and the purpose of the preen oil a bird takes from its uropygial gland just above its 'parson's nose', the base of its tail. Feathers are designed to be waterproof without the addition of any oil, not even preen oil, which I take to be only a sort of conditioner allowing for a smoother passage of the feather being preened through the bird's beak. It's those interlocking barbules and underlying down feathers that provide both waterproofing and weatherproofing. The merest hint of oil or detergent breaks through the barrier, leaving a gap where water can get through to chill the bird, especially as the down feathers act as a sponge, soaking up more and more water until the bird is completely saturated.

So, in order to wash an oiled bird effectively, we must remove not only every trace of oil, but also every trace of the product we used to wash them with. Using the system devised for oiled sea birds we can save oiled garden birds and release them, fully recovered, within days.

When an oiled garden bird falls into your lap do not attempt to wash it for at least twenty-four hours. The only initial treatment required is to clean its eyes, nose, beak and vent gently with a paper towel. Apply our old friend chloramphenicol ointment to the eyes in case they have been burnt by the oil and feed the bird a part of a Kaobiotic tablet by Upjohn, once again available from your vet. The dose rate is a whole tablet for a sea bird, so our garden birds would require the merest splinter. Give it every day until you are satisfied that any oil it may have swallowed while preening has cleared from its digestive system. Try to encourage the bird to feed, as anything passing through that embattled digestive system will help stem any dangerous enteritis.

Keep the bird in a warm closed-in cage, remember its built-in blanket of down feathers is now useless, offering no warmth whatsoever.

On the following day, provided your bird looks composed and steady, mix up two per cent of Fairy Liquid washing-up liquid in water at 45°C. Next, immerse your bird; head, of course, above the water, in the warm solution for ten seconds only. Work the solution into and under all the bird's feathers, cleaning

the head feathers with a small Oral-B tooth-brush. Provided the solution is at the correct strength and temperature, the oil will surprise you as it quickly falls away from the feathers. If the oil is really thick then use other clean baths of the same solution until you are satis-fied that all the oil is loosened.

Now comes the most important part of the process – the rinsing. Using a plastic spray attachment for taps, spray the bird with clear water, once again at 45°C, just hot enough for you to hold your hands in comfortably. Direct the jet up and under all the feathers and keep rinsing until little beads of water start to form on the feathers. It may take a considerable time but, amazingly, the more you rinse the feathers the drier they become. At the end of the process your bird should look completely dry with the typically dry fluffy appearance of any garden bird. Put it under an infra-red lamp for twenty-four hours where it can preen each feather back into shape and it will be ready for release three or four days later. Never try to dry your washed bird with a towel – it only adds to the contamination.

We did not have to bathe our starlings and pigeons, even though they were filthy. We knew that they would all have to stay with us for at least six months until they had moulted out all those burnt feathers. Our only hope was that none of the feather follicles suffered damage in the blast.

Our mini production line treating the hundreds of casualties from the factory

Dehydration

By this time everybody was getting filthy dirty handling so many sooty birds. And when it came to the next stage, the gavaging (see 'Fluids', Chapter 11), the state of Sue and volunteers Lynne Kuschel, Mary Jellis and Chris Patterson, who had the mucky task, had to be seen to be believed. The gavaging was probably the most important aspect of that first night's treatment. Dehydration, which we were countering, is one of the most potent killers of small birds, and is brought on not just by the lack of moisture but, more spec-tacularly, by the kind of trauma these birds had suffered. Sue, being my long-suffering partner, has gavaged many birds before, but for Lynne, Mary and Chris it was a first time. But once the technique was explained, they had no trouble in syringing 5ml of Lectade into each of their quota of birds.

Gavaging with fluids is often the rec-ommended method of treating a bird that is dehydrated. However, it needs a fair amount of training and practise and should really be left to those who would like to take in more bird casualties. For this reason I will include some details of fluid therapy in the next chap-ter. Suffice it to say, if you have an injured bird and you do not want to get involved in gavaging, then DO NOT attempt to trickle anything to drink into its beak – you will probably drown the bird. If the bird is aware and can lift its head, then simply put a small bowl of Lectade or International Rehydrating

A blue tit in the hand

Fluid with the bird and let it get its own drink. Pushing its beak into the fluid just once will show the bird where the drink is; the bird will do the rest.

Never offer a compromised bird water to drink. International Rehydrating Fluid can be mixed from the ingredients in any kitchen cupboard and will often save a bird's life. To mix it, take one tablespoon of sugar (exact measurements, please) and one teaspoon of salt and mix it thoroughly into a litre of warm water. The fluid should be discarded after twenty-four hours and fresh fluid mixed if your casualty still looks poorly. If it's up on its

---

International Rehydrating Fluid

(Isotonic)

1 tablespoon sugar

1 teaspoon salt

1 litre warm water

May be used as an emergency fluid. Do not use plain water, as this can make a dehydrated bird's condition worse.

---

feet and bright then it can take water alone.

At the end of our rescue production line, young Melissa Meons, one of our Saturday morning, teenage volunteers who had stayed all day, and night for that matter, sorted the birds into warm cages with shallow bowls of Lectade to drink, corn for the pigeons and clean white maggots for the starlings.

We made sure that our packed cages only had shallow dishes of Lectade for, knowing a starling's propensity for bathing and the state of our mucky lot, the bowls would have soon become full of black and sticky mud.

During all this, I was busy setting up a fracture clinic and any birds with injuries, notably beak losses, were passed to me for assessment and treatment which would need the experiences I had gained over many years of dealing with broken wings, beaks and legs in garden birds. Fractures are strictly the domain of the more experienced bird handler and should be referred to a wildlife centre or experienced vet.

11 Complications

Other than the procedures I have described, particularly capture, antibiotics and simple eye treatment, most other involvement with injured wild birds requires more technically difficult regimes that are only suitable for those with an interest in more than just one bird casualty. Most of the injuries described in this chapter demand the skills of the more experienced person; alternatively the bird should be taken to a wildlife centre or veterinary surgeon with an interest in birds.

I had been dealing with avian fractures for years, so it was my job on the production line to assess and deal with any leg, wing or beak fractures.

Leg fractures

I had settled myself down at a small table surrounded by bandages, tapes, Weetabix packets and – most important of all – a small selection of bamboo canes with which to splint the broken legs.

As the birds were passed to me it soon became obvious that most were suffering from leg fractures caused by the fall from the top of the devastated building. With any leg fracture in any bird I always find it imperative to dive in and sort it out before the bird has any chance to do any more damage.

Birds will think nothing of hopping around on a broken leg, often forcing any shattered bones through the skin, introducing infection to the fracture site and making healing so much more difficult. In general, the bones of a bird heal and mend very quickly, but they may deteriorate and never heal if there is any infection present.

Many people bring birds to the hospital assuming that because a bird can't stand it must have a broken leg. True, this could be the case, but more often there is just a temporary paralysis caused by a concussion, a vitamin deficiency or simply a pulled muscle, all of which will resolve themselves with cage rest and a vitamin-enriched diet. Sometimes, however, especially in the corvids, the legs are permanently twisted or bent out of shape. This is invariably found in young birds and is

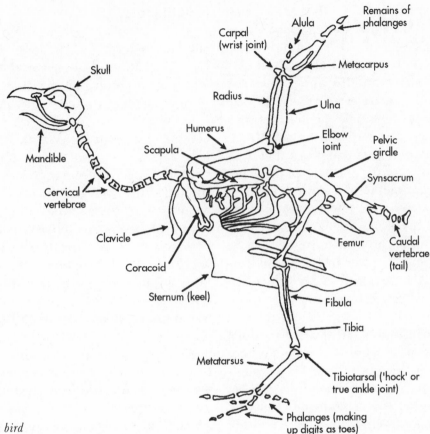

Skull

Carpal
(wrist joint)

Alula

Remains of
phalanges

Metacarpus

Radius

Ulna

Humerus

Elbow
joint

Pelvic
girdle

Mandible

Scapula

Synsacrum

Cervical
vertebrae

Clavicle

Femur

Caudal
vertebrae
(tail)

Coracoid

Sternum (keel)

Fibula

Tibia

Metatarsus

Tibiotarsal ('hock' or
true ankle joint)

Phalanges (making
up digits as toes)

The skeleton of a bird

labelled metabolic bone disease. Sadly, there is seldom a way to rectify the deformities, which often necessitate euthanasia by the vet.

A genuine fracture is usually very obvious. The bird will have no control over the part of the leg below the fracture, which will hang loosely, often twisted out of line with the rest of the limb. On holding the leg you will be able to feel 'crepitus' as the two broken ends touch. Don't be alarmed, there will not be the excruciating pain you would expect in a human or other mammal; birds seem to have hardly any sensation of pain at a fracture site, an added bonus when it comes to setting the leg – that is, reducing the fracture until the broken bone is, more or less, back in direct alignment. Normally this would be done under anaesthetic, but I am sure that more birds die from anaesthesia than any other surgical procedure, so if your patient shows no discomfort you can safely splint the leg with no further risk. Occasionally, a bird may wince as you touch a fracture and in this case anaesthesia will have to be resorted to as local analgesics do not seem to be effective in birds.

Always handle the bird gently but firmly, preventing it flapping its wings or, of course, kicking its legs. Lay it on a heat pad, or hot water bottle wrapped with a cloth, and cover the bird with a thick towel, effectively cutting out all light and keeping the bird under control. If at any time the bird starts to breathe extra heavily and gasp for breath, then stop what you are doing immediately, place the bird in a warm dark box and try again in a couple of hours.

With the bird settled and quiet, feel along the broken leg until you touch the fracture and then once again, gently but firmly, reduce the fracture, making sure that the foot is in line with the other foot. I know of a vet who once reduced the fracture on a budgerigar's leg so that it healed with the foot on backwards. So make sure it is round the right way at this stage. Reducing involves pulling the leg below the fracture until the two ends of the broken bone meet in alignment. Once again, if the bird shows any sign of discomfort stop what you are doing and try later.

If there is any breakage in the skin, bathe the wound with dilute Savlon or Hibiscrub followed, over the next five days, by a course of antibiotics.

The next task is to immobilise the fracture site completely. This is done with a strip of bamboo cane cut to a suitable length and width. Bamboo is ideal because it can be cut to suit any leg fracture and has a grooved interior ideal for siting a small bird's leg. Keeping the splint clear of the joints, if practical, helps keep those joints mobile.

Once the part of the leg with the fracture is nestled into the bamboo splint, wrap it around with 1 cm zinc oxide plaster tape (available from any chemist). As the most common fractures are to the tibia, or upper leg, I also flex the leg below the tibiotarsal, or hock, joint to 90°, holding it in position with one strip of zinc oxide plaster. This flexing of the lower leg helps keep the tibia in the right position.

Remove the splint after seven days – birds heal very rapidly – and check the fracture site for movement. If there is still a slight instability then re-splint the bone for another seven days, but leave any joints free for movement. Any further restriction of the joints may result in an arthritis and permanent disability. If the leg or joints do appear stiff, then some gentle physiotherapy should still enable you to release the bird after a couple of weeks' convalescence in a flight cage.

Flexing the leg joint through 90° will help a broken leg to heal in the right position

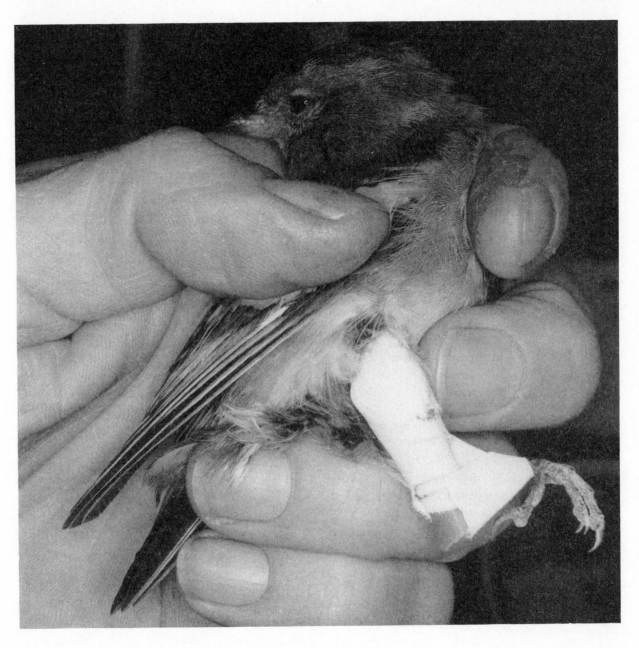

It all sounds fairly simple, doesn't it? However, birds are not always that co-operative and fractures may be near a joint, or there may be more than one fracture, or both legs may be broken. In all these cases, think about it carefully before taking any action and improvise if necessary.

When I first started taking in casualties there were no guidelines and every treatment was improvisation, but it worked. I think my classic improvisation was to cope with birds suffering from two broken legs. Having splinted the legs I had to keep the bird from putting any weight on them until the fractures had healed. My solution was to build a wooden frame from which I could suspend the bird with zinc oxide tape until I judged that the legs were strong enough to bear weight. Each time I use the system it takes some time to adjust the straps and feeding bowls for each individual bird, but it works and is worth the perseverance.

Sometimes, even with the best of attention, a broken leg will not mend or the blood and nerve supply below the fracture has been compromised. If the lower part of the leg is dry, stiff and obviously dead, then tie a piece of thread, tightly, around where it meets live tissue and eventually it will simply snap off. If the lower leg is useless but still obviously alive and if it impedes the bird's movement, then an experienced veterinary surgeon should carry out the amputation. Most birds will manage normally with one leg – no doubt you have seen the occasional one-legged blackbird or pigeon visit your garden. They are usually the survivors of encounters with fishing lines or the black cotton put over fruit crops.

You will also, unfortunately, see garden birds with these horrifying ligatures still in place acting like tourniquets, slowly and re-morselessly killing off the bird's legs and feet. If you can, catch any affected bird and remove *every* trace of cutting line.

It is essential to remove every trace of the ligature, which often involves digging deep into the wounds with forceps and gradually loosening the line until it can be fully un-wound. Don't actually cut the line, but search for the loose end and gradually pull the whole length free, making sure you have it all. Often, a magnifying glass will help find very fine line, sometimes really deep inside the wounds.

Quite often the wounds will bleed, some-times copiously, but dabbing them with a pad of gauze soaked in dilute Savlon should stop the flow. Give any birds which have bled Lectade to drink for the first few days and keep *any* patient for at least two weeks, just to make sure there are no pieces of line you might have missed.

There will also be horrifying cases involv-ing birds with line wrapped around their tongues. Unravel it as you would from around a leg and, once again, give the bird two weeks to recover.

Often the leg or foot below the ligature will drop off; but as I have said earlier, most birds,

A bird with its beak open like this usually has damage to the axis point. The feather has stuck to its tongue and it cannot release it

except perhaps swans and birds of prey, will manage quite nicely on just one. If a bird loses both legs or both feet, then I think that there is no alternative other than euthanasia by a vet.

I am opposed to the too easy option of 'putting a bird out of its misery', when care and knowledge could save it. However, a bird that cannot perch would, in no time, suffer contamination and the ensuing disease to its underside would lead gradually to a deterioration until the bird died naturally, in this case suffering miserably first.

Dislocations

Sometimes, especially with blackbirds, and moorhens if you live near water, any apparent fracture may well be a dislocation, sometimes compounded, of the hock joint. If any suspected fracture is near the joint, feel the ends of the bones and if they seem smooth and rounded, just like the ends of a dog's marrow bone meal, then more than likely your fracture is a dislocation. Should it be compounded, you will be able to see the undamaged ends.

Once again, cover the bird with a towel and manipulate the joint back into place – the smooth top of the metatarsus should fit into the slight cup at the bottom of the tibia. A compound dislocation should, first of all, be thoroughly cleaned with dilute Savlon or Hibiscrub. Any skin tears can be lightly sutured with one or two stitches. Apply a light strapping for a few days then the leg should function normally again.

Broken wings

Luckily, only one of the birds at the explosion site, a pigeon, had a broken wing. It was presumably incurred when the bird collided with a ledge as it vainly tried to fly in its plummet to the ground. Fractures of the wing have to be immobilised, just like leg fractures; the contours of the wings and the presence of feathers make the process a little more complicated but it can be carried out successfully. Mind you, failure means a grounded bird that must be looked after for the rest of its life and some wings are so hopelessly broken, often aggravated by the bird continuing to flap, that there is no way it will ever heal.

A common cause of wing fractures in garden birds is damage by an air gun pellet. If parents could only see how an air gun pellet shatters through a bird's bones then perhaps they would think twice before letting their children have such a lethal weapon.

Simple and compounded fractures occur at three sites: the humerus; the radius and ulna; and the metacarpus, which I call 'the fingers', roughly the same bones we have in our own arms.

The most depressing of these is invariably a fracture, or often multiple fracture, of the humerus – the large bone that, if you like, runs from the shoulder to the elbow. An added complication is that, in a bird, the humerus is hollow and forms part of the respiratory system. Not only that, but when it breaks and the bird continues flapping, its sharp edges tear the overlying tissue to shreds.

In larger birds – sparrowhawk-size and upwards – we have been successful in using surgical wire to stabilise a fractured humerus. But as this involves anaesthesia it really is not practical for our small garden birds.

There isn't the same urgency as there is when dealing with a leg fracture. Rather, a bird with a wing injury should be left for twenty-four hours to give the bird a better chance to settle. Close confinement in a dark hospital cage will stop the bird causing any more damage, although a light wrapping round with a cohesive flexible bandage will make absolutely sure. This new concept in bandaging, known as Co-Flex by Millpledge, available through vets, is ideal for birds as it will not adhere to or damage any feathers, although care must be taken if it is used across the chest because it may constrict the breathing.

Owing to the position of the humerus, it is often impossible to splint a fracture and, as internal fixation is out of the question in small birds, I have found that to do nothing other than confine the bird in peace and quiet is the most effective remedy. You can strap the wing to the body but I find that birds will struggle against any restriction of their wings and the sheer power of the shoulder muscles will continually pull the proximal part of the humerus away from the rest. With close confinement and no external stimuli the bird will not want to use its wings, giving the fracture time to callous, often within a few days.

The radius and the ulna, between the elbow and the wrist (the carpal joint) are much more accessible and can be splinted easily. They are two bones running parallel and if only one is broken then the other acts as a natural splint, needing no interference from us other than to keep the bird confined and quiet for about a week.

However, it is usually the case that both bones are broken, in which case we do need to interfere, normally applying a splint fashioned from cardboard. I have dealt with many radius/ulna fractures and I have found that cereal packets, in my case Weetabix packets, are easily shaped and are neither too heavy nor too light for the purpose. Cut out a cardboard shape like a narrow egg-timer (or the kind of bowtie with curved edges), which when folded in two looks about the right size for your bird's wing.

Firstly align the fractured ulna, the thickest of the two bones, making sure that the wing is in its correct position. Then, with your Weetabix splint folded at its narrowest point, slide it, following the contours of the wing, over the fracture site, held stable by gripping the cardboard. Still holding the fracture inside the splint, wrap the whole thing securely with Co-Flex bandage. Once again, to prevent problems with any joints, remove the splint in seven days when the fracture should have stabilised. Another seven days in close confinement will prevent any relapses.

Fractures to the metacarpus are usually compounded and are usually very close to the carpal joint. After cleaning and closing any wounds, simply splint the whole wing using the radius/ulna splint technique, but this time check for success after only four days, resplinting for another four days if there is no marked stability.

*

For some reason broken beaks seem most common on blackbirds

The pigeon with the broken wing at the cement works had a fracture to his carpal joint, but when splinted was stable enough to join the others.

It was beginning to appear that for some reason the explosion had instigated some form of ominous, hidden problems with the birds' beaks, legs and feet. It seemed as though, in that split second, the blood circulating to those exposed areas was severely damaged. I have had exhaustive tests done by John Cooper, the country's leading pathologist, but still the horror of that moment defies explanation. I have already shocked you with stories of beaks falling off and my sticking them back on with tissue glue, but just a few days later, and even more horrifyingly, some of the birds' feet and legs started to wither and break off, completely dead. There was no explanation and nothing we could do as these little birds – it only seemed to have affected the starlings – gradually became crippled. Some were lucky and only lost one leg or foot or just a toe, but those with more debilitating damage had to go to the vet. I had read somewhere about a goose with artificial feet, but there was nothing I could do for these birds.

Happily, the surrogate beaks I had stuck on seemed to be working. Nobody could tell me what would happen next but, miraculously, a new beak sheath seemed to grow underneath the prostheses, gradually pushing the false beak off and revealing a perfectly usable starling beak. The pigeons never grew new beaks and now live at the hospital, sporting tiny little stumps of beaks. They have formed a little colony and seem to manage very well. Even old Stumpy, who lost not only his beak but one leg as well, joins in the flurry to feed and squabble in true pigeon fashion.

Fluids and Gavaging

I am convinced that the gavaging of fluids saved the birds in that fateful incident. I have, on many occasions, seen an apparently dying bird up on its feet within half an hour of an infusion of fluid; so I would highly recommend that, although the problems of tonicity in fluids may seem complex and the actual gavaging traumatic, this technique should be learnt as a sure-fire method of doubling your success rate in an instant.

It's important to understand the reason for fluid imbalance, or dehydration as it is more popularly known. Suffice it to say that in a body's metabolism, fluids are kept at equal levels inside and outside the cells by a process called osmosis. Loss of extracellular fluids by bleeding, vomiting, diarrhoea and other factors will cause intracellular fluids to drain from the cells. Fluids available are either isotonic, which, if you like, is 'osmosis friendly', or hyper- or hypotonic, which can damage cells. It is simplest to stick to isotonic fluids, which can be administered by all routes: intravenously, orally, or subcutaneously. There seems to be a dearth of literature in Britain but, as I understand it, there are two types of fluid which can do little harm. These are Hartmann's Solution, which closely resembles extracellular fluid for first-level application to replace sodium, potassium, calcium, bicarbonate and chloride leached from the cells, followed by dextrose/saline (in fact, sodium chloride and glucose 4%) for maintenance of the 'patient'.

Subcutaneous fluids for birds can be administered at a rough guide of five per cent of body weight; for example, a bird weighing 150 grams can have 7.5 millilitres of fluid every six hours. The route of administration I would recommend is just under the skin to the right (that is the bird's right) of its breastbone or keel. Just below the skin at this point is the large muscle mass that propels the wings and there is little chance of damaging any important organ or vessel. Inject the fluids in small amounts to prevent stretching the skin and causing patches of skin to die off.

These subcutaneous fluids take some time to be absorbed. A more hazardous but quicker route is by gavaging straight into the proventriculus, the bird's equivalent of a stomach. You are now probably flummoxed by the word 'gavage' and will be horrified to find out, if you look it up in a dictionary, that it is the method of force-feeding unfortunate geese to produce that distasteful abomination, pâté de foie gras. It is the same method of application of food or fluids to a debilitated bird, but carried out with compassion and a regard for the feelings of the bird. And it is going to save the bird's life.

Before even attempting to gavage a bird, especially the small garden birds we are concerned with, make yourself familiar with the layout of a bird's mouth, throat, oesophagus, crop, proventriculus and gizzard. You should notice that immediately behind the tongue is a hole that constantly opens and closes. This is the glottis, the opening of the trachea and lungs. Any fluid at all that spills into this opening will cause pneumonia and usually the death of the bird. The task is to get the right amount of fluids safely past the glottis

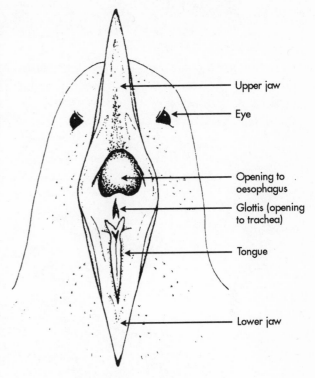

Bird with beak open, showing glottis

down the back of the throat and into the proventriculus. Incidentally, when I say fluids, I do not mean whisky, brandy, milk or grandma's old remedy, those are all surefire killers of dehydrated birds – as is water, because it is hypotonic, meaning it can actually accelerate the processes of dehydration and resultant cell damage.

It takes a lot of experience to be able to evaluate the degree of dehydration in an avian patient, so let us assume that any bird you are

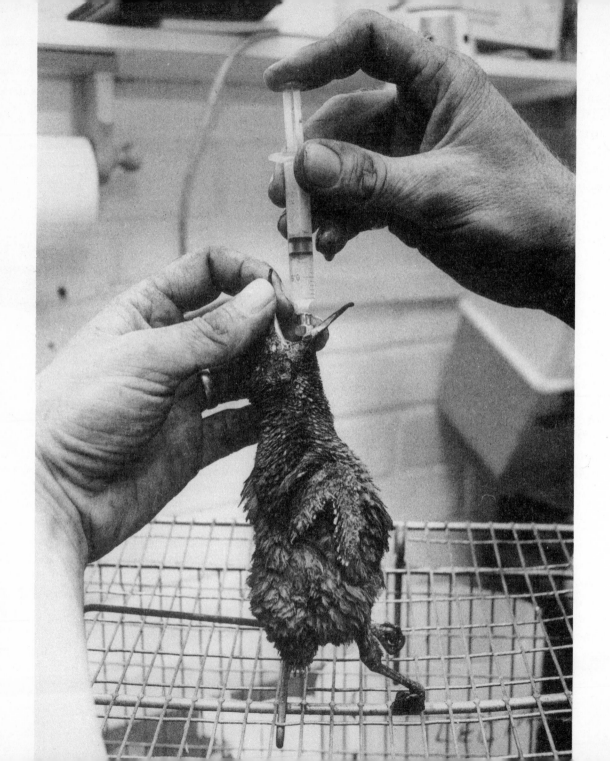

able to pick up is suffering some form of fluid imbalance. In keeping with this assumption, any new patient should only be offered iso-tonic fluids, with the solution of choice being Lectade, manufactured by Smith-Kline Bee-cham, and available from your vet. Lectade is not going to feed your bird, but it will halt the downward spiral so that, after a few hours, liquid nutrition can be offered. I can only stress that solid food at the beginning will add to the bird's problems.

Gavaging a new casualty, provided that it is carried out very carefully, will often save a bird's life, but please remember that it is a fairly drastic solution and that things can go wrong, jeopardising all your good intentions towards your patient. However, take it very carefully and you will be amazed at the re-cuperative properties of just a few millilitres of fluid.

To be prepared to treat various small birds you will need to carry a selection of soft rubber tubes with rounded ends that will fit on to the standard luer fitting of 2, 5 or 10 ml syringes. The thickness of the tubes can be estimated by imagining that it has to pass down a bird's throat and through its oesophagus. For small birds like sparrows, starlings, blackbirds and thrushes we use Spreull's needles of various lengths, once again obtainable through a vet-erinary practice or medical suppliers. Spreull's needles are in fact metal tubes with a

Gavaging fluids to one of the injured starlings

bulbous, blunt end that are manufactured to fit on to the standard luer fittings of syringes. (Luer is the description of the stub of the syringe where the needle fits.)

Firstly, mix some Lectade with warm water and then draw the amount you think the bird can take into the syringe. For instance, let's say 5 millilitres for a starling. Fit your Spreull's needle and then lubricate it with a minimum amount of liquid paraffin. Then, taking the bird in your left hand, calculate how much of the Spreull's needle will need to go into the bird to reach its proventriculus – which is about level and behind the bottom of its sternum, the breastbone.

Open the bird's beak and insert the Spreull's needle, or tube, into the bird's throat, making sure to miss the tracheal open-ing immediately behind the tongue.

Supporting the bird by its head or the base of the beak straightens the neck so that the tube can be slid slowly down into the crop and oesophagus until it stops. If it does not appear to be far enough in, *do not push* it any further, but wiggle it around a little bit until you feel it pass the obstruction. Any unnecessary press-ure may result in puncturing the crop or oesophagus, a complication the bird can well do without.

Once you are satisfied that it is in position, and keeping the beak open, slowly depress the syringe to release the fluids. Keeping the beak open will enable you to see if there is an overflow back towards the trachea. If there is,

Even small birds can be helped with a little suturing

sheet aluminium if you are metal-minded. It needs to be maintained at quite a high temperature, far higher than required by mammals. About 30°C seems acceptable, but I always feel that the bird itself is the best barometer – a bird that is cold to the touch will not recover, whilst a warm bird will soon be on its feet struggling to escape.

There is the flippant saying about a dead bird with its feet in the air. In fact, this is not far from the truth, as a bird lying on its back will suffer with respiratory difficulties and impaired circulation. Always put a bird on its keel, if necessary making a little cradle out of a rolled towel.

remove the tube and place the bird upright in a warm position until the crisis has passed.

Repeat the procedure every couple of hours until the bird appears stronger and can take Lectade from a bowl placed inside its cage. A bird can be gavaged up to 50 millilitres per kilogram of body weight every six to eight hours.

Aftercare

The ideal warm position for a bird needing this kind of attention, that is, one that is unable to stand and nourish itself, is in a hospital cage. There are only a few hospital cage designs on the market but I have one, from the now defunct Reliable Thermostat Co., which seems to be the most efficient and can be quite easily reproduced in timber, or in

Gavage and warmth were the lifesavers when we brought back the first wave of starlings and pigeons devastated by the explosion at Pitstone. Although there were only a few patients in the beginning, we knew that there were bound to be many more, so we called in extra volunteers and briefed them on gavage. Before long they were all syringing fluids into starlings as though they had been doing it for years.

We worked all night after that first fateful day of the explosion but at first light the following day Nigel and Colin went back to the cement works to see if there were any stragglers we had missed. This time, however, they were not allowed inside the building, which had been deemed unsafe. Thankfully the workers at the site had completed one last round-up of a couple of dozen more casualties, the last we ever found there. We never did find the kestrel.

The whole exercise turned out to be a crash course in how to treat most garden bird casualties. There really are only two other incidents that are likely to occur in the garden but do always be prepared for the unexpected.

Drowning

The first of the two other common incidents is drowning in the garden pool or the birdbath if it is too deep. Never give up on an apparently drowned bird, but turn it upside down to shake any water from its mouth and trachea and then put it somewhere warm and pray for a miracle. It's surprising how many dead birds have come to life with a little drying and warming.

The other incident doesn't really involve a garden bird, although it occurs in your garden. You may suddenly see a ringed racing pigeon sitting all forlorn under the bird table with an apparent inability to fly. There is usually nothing wrong with the bird other than tiredness and hunger as some racing pigeons are let free hungry in the hope that they will fly home for food. Some don't make it. Hence the enormous feral pigeon populations around the world. Anyway, should you meet a crashed racing pigeon, give it food and shelter for a few days and it will be on its way.

Incidentally, racing pigeon owners are supposed to rubber stamp their name, address and telephone number on the bird's flight feathers. It is sometimes worth a phone call although often to be told that the owner does not want the pigeon back. Another feral to join the millions.

No garden, it seems would be complete without its quota of baby birds, most of which are not injured and most are not even orphaned. It's these baby birds, orphans, that take over most summers at the hospital. They are demanding from dawn till dusk and are such a major headache that they demand a chapter all to themselves.

12 Hatchling, Nestling and Fledgling

My first attempts at encouraging birds to breed in my garden never turned out the way I wanted them to. We lived, at the time, backing on to the New Malden golf course, which boasted a whole range of species from crows down to long-tailed tits. I decided to make some nest boxes but, having no reference material, fell at the first hurdle. Luckily, the birds themselves improvised and thanks to them my efforts bore fruit.

The first classic mistake was to build a very elaborate bird table with a nest box in the roof. Almost instantly, the box was taken over by a pair of starlings who effectively prohibited any other birds feeding at the table.

At the bottom of the garden, right next to the golf course, I erected a blue tit nest box but the hole was too big and a pair of great tits were soon in residence.

Every day I would walk past the boxes, never daring to look in but ever hoping for some sign to let me know there was a family in one or the other. I need not have bothered for, on the day when the eggs must have hatched, each arrival of a parent was greeted by excited baby calls that I could hear from the back door.

At first I could see nothing through the entrance holes, but just a cursory tap on the box would be answered by a clamour of squeaks from within. Eventually I could see the open beaks as I tapped and then heads were stuck out of the holes, only to panic back inside when they saw me standing there.

Then one day the tit box was silent and empty. They had all flown before I was out of bed that morning. The starlings stayed at home for a few more days, but as they emerged for their first flights, mum and dad sat on the chain-link fence calling to them in that funny, rough little warble starlings have.

None of them made a mistake and all four were soon lined up on the fence, mouths open at their parents, demanding to be fed. They stayed around for about a week and each time an adult starling flew into the garden, behind it would be flying two or three open-mouthed clamouring youngsters.

Starlings are lucky – they fly straight from the nest. Other youngsters, like blackbirds, almost fall out and then learn their flying skills over the next few days. It's these probationary baby birds that are looked on, by us, as orphans and who turn up at the hospital by the dozen.

There should always be that quandary whether to 'rescue' an apparently orphaned wild bird or to leave it to its own and its parents' devices. It's often all too easy to pick up a helpless fledgling but, knowing the difficulty in hand-rearing a wild bird, would it be better off left alone? Assuming, that is, it is left alone, for invariably the mother or father are waiting in the wings for your departure, when they will swoop down and succour their off-spring far more successfully than you or I could ever do.

Young birds are often out of their nest but are seldom in trouble unless they are threatened by a predator, whether from a wild or a domestic source. Then a timely rescue could save the youngster's life. However, remember that to the bird you are merely another predator, not the 'knight in shining armour' you think you are, so do not expect any thanks or co-operation from your 'damsel in distress'. It will often scream, flap and peck until you quieten it by putting it into a dark box. Similarly, a young bird exposed to a heavy shower of rain needs rescuing. Mind you, after this foundling has been dried and warmed either in front of an electric fire or with a warm hairdryer, it can be returned to its original perching place once the bad weather has abated. There is still the misconception that the 'human scent' will deter the parents, but birds have little or no sense of smell and will usually carry on feeding their progeny as if nothing had happened. We have arranged successful reunions after two or three days, with the doting parents proving far more dependable than the brooding hen so easily put off a nest of eggs.

Many people phone our 'help-line' telling of orphaned birds they had rescued, often twenty-four hours earlier. It's only when the youngster constantly refuses to feed that they eventually telephone us in desperation. Our advice is to put the bird back outside, where it was found; either inside an open cardboard box or in an old bird cage, both partially covered to offer some protection from the sun. In most cases the parents are still in the vicinity and will soon respond to the insistent hungry calls of their own youngster, a fledgling which is perfectly at ease outside the confines of its nest cup or nest box. Fledglings, with the exception of house martins, never return to their nest of their own accord once they have left. House martin fledglings sometimes come out of the nest prematurely and will appreciate being returned to their nest cup in the eaves. And, even if you cannot identify their particular nest site, any nest cup with youngsters of a similar age will suffice as a foster home until they are all ready to start their flying lessons in earnest.

Fledglings, in the main, are feathered and close to flying, but hatchlings and nestlings are particularly vulnerable outside their nests and should be returned there rather than taking the drastic step of adopting them for hand-rearing. Young birds from the egg to self-sufficiency go through various stages of development, all of which demand different approaches should we have to get involved in their welfare.

Eggs

Even the birds' eggs cause concern, and many people phone me distressed that something has gone wrong with the blackbird's nest in their hedge. The facts of egg-laying and incubation are poorly understood and even I, as a boy on my excursions over Wimbledon Common, used to assume that a nest containing cold eggs had been deserted. Not so. I now realise that a cold egg is not necessarily a dead egg.

A female garden bird, let's say that blackbird in the hedge, will lay a single egg each day for three to seven days. She will not start to brood – that is, sit on the eggs and warm them – until the complete clutch is laid. Until that moment the eggs will remain cold and undeveloped, but they will still be fertile. Only when the hen blackbird starts to warm them, with the freshly plucked brood patch on

An orphaned chaffinch

her abdomen will the embryos start to develop. The brood patch is a piece of bare skin on the hen's abdomen warmed by extra blood vessels just for the purpose of providing the heat necessary to maintain a regular development of the eggs for the two-week incubation period. If, for any reason during that two weeks, the eggs are chilled, then their development will cease and the embryos die. This is probably the main reason why a sitting bird should never be disturbed. She may leave and then return to re-warm the eggs and only some days later will realise they are not going to hatch. She will then desert and start nest-building and laying, all over again, at a different site.

The cock bird has little to do with the incubation of the eggs and will never attempt to hatch them should anything happen to his mate. We should adopt the same attitude and ignore cold eggs, no matter how they have become cold. They may be newly laid or may be deserted, but even then I regard it as a futile exercise to hatch the eggs of garden birds and try to rear the helpless hatchlings, even if the removal of eggs from a nest was not against the law.

However, when the hen dies while brooding over newly-hatched youngsters, they too will perish because the cock bird will not keep them warm. Only then will I make an attempt at hand-rearing them, on the assumption that

Some baby birds – 'plastics' – are tiny and unidentifiable

they have had at least some initial feeding from their parents.

Hatchlings

The baby garden bird, just hatched from the egg, will never win any beauty contest – its eyes are closed as two bulges on its head; its abdomen is distended, giving a transparent view of its internal working parts and its beak is flanked by distinctive phalanges of species-specific bright colours. These bright colours – for instance, deep red and orange with white edges in a chaffinch – are designed to attract attention, and of course feeding, by the adults of the same species. For some reason the 'gape' of the young cuckoo, a vivid deep orange with yellow phalanges, attracts all manner of foster parents as well as its own kind.

Some of the newly hatched garden birds have a few tufts of down on their heads, but the rest of the body is completely naked with a distinct pink, shiny appearance, earning them the title of 'plastics' at St Tiggywinkles. In fact, until they grow their first feathers, they are hatchlings and need warmth and protection from chills. If they become cold they will not respond to feeding stimuli and will soon perish.

Sometimes these 'plastics' need rescuing: when the hen parent has been postitively identified as dead or when the nest is built in an exposed position and is seriously damaged by rain, for instance. The family cat often

---

Recipe for Wildlife Hospital Trust Glop

- cup Pedigree Chum Puppy food
- cup Dried Insect Food (Sluis Universal or Haiths Prosecto)
- cup cold water
- half-teaspoon multi-vitamin powder (SA37 or Millpledge Vetamin)
- quarter-teaspoon bone meal feed
- quarter-teaspoon Can-Addase Enzyme (available through vets)

Liquidise till smooth and the consistency of soft ice cream. Should be discarded after 24 hours.

---

comes home proudly bearing its freshly caught plastic which, apart from needing the obligatory antibiotic injection, is usually undamaged. It's pointless putting it back in the nest as the cat will only return to reclaim its trophy. In fact, it will probably gradually empty the nest, so if you can follow your cat after its first foray, it would be a good idea to protect the rest of the hatchlings with a wire-netting screen slung across at cat access points.

Other plastics, usually sparrows, although the identification of individuals even by their coloured gape is not easy, will suddenly appear, helpless, in the middle of a lawn or path nowhere near any nest sites. There is no reason for them being there and as there is no convenient nest site nearby, they do need to be adopted and hand-reared, a not-always rewarding task.

Luckily most garden birds, whether they are seed-eaters or insectivores as adults, are reared, in the wild, on a high protein diet of insects, spiders, grubs and other creepy-crawlies which, in the bird nursery, is easily supplemented by a mixture we call St Tiggy-winkles Glop. Only when they reach the fledgling stage do they need to be offered adult food in the form of seeds or insects as their own particular species prefers. The exceptions – although the collared dove is the only true garden bird amongst them – are the pigeons, doves and birds of prey which all require more specialised feeding practices.

In spite of all our experience in rearing hatchlings, we still strive, whenever possible, to get them back to their nests. House martin 'plastics' are always landing on somebody's path as their nests fall from their precarious fixings in the eaves. However, a prefabricated nest can easily be fashioned from a plastic flower pot with a notch the size of a fifty-pence piece in the rim. Lined with paper towel and nailed on the original site of the fallen nest, with the babies *in situ*, it will in no time be a hive of activity as adult martins return to their parental duties.

If you do manage to return a hatchling to its parents, then you have saved yourself weeks

A nestling blackbird shares a towel-lined box with a nestling thrush

of hand-feeding and the added worry of having such a tiny, frail creature fully reliant on you for its existence. However, if, in spite of all your precautions and efforts you still have a plastic which needs hand-rearing, then be prepared to devote every waking moment to your ever-insistent orphan.

Looking after an orphan hatchling

First of all, your foster baby will be cold and probably dehydrated. If it has no feathers then it will need to be kept in a box on a radiator at a constant ambient temperature of between 30° and 32°C. When the first feathers have grown through, about a week later, a regular temperature of 21° to 27°C will suffice. However, never trust your thermometer and always double check by feeling the bird – it should always feel warm to the touch, never hot and never cold. You will soon become experienced enough to recognise when your bird is feeling comfortable – for one thing, it will only then demand feeding.

I am a great believer in administering fluids to any newly arrived baby bird. These can either be subcutaneous fluids or my preferred method of gavage with warmed Lectade. A Spreulls needle fitted to a 2 ml syringe is ideal for gavage of a baby bird and can quite easily, but gently, be slid down into the crop and proventriculus. Once again the simple formula for fluid requirements is five per cent of body weight. This means that a 10 gm baby bird should receive 0.05 ml of Lectade,

although by observing the crop filling you may be able to get a little more in before it floods back into the tracheal opening, the glottis, just behind the tongue. *Most newly taken-in baby birds are killed by drowning, with that first drink, so be extra careful and, if in doubt, don't give any fluids. In any case never, ever, give water, milk, brandy or whisky – all of which will probably kill your bird even if they do not get into their lungs. If* you are at all worried about giving fluids by gavage or injection, then it is safest not to give anything.

In its new, warm quarters the baby bird should be kept in a clean, small, cup-shaped receptacle, such as an old margarine tub. This 'nest' should be lined with paper towel to give the baby support and that feeling of security that a close-fitting nest gives in the wild. Do not use old birds' nests, they will be dirty and contain some parasites and soon become soiled with faeces and splattered food. The paper towel in the margarine tub can be changed regularly to give your baby bird the best chance possible. Just remember that the odds are stacked against its survival, and take every opportunity to prevent infection or, worst of all, fungus from old nests, gaining a foothold.

Once your orphan has warmed, any slight noise or movement will prompt the 'feed-me' response – a vast, gaping mouth, larger than the head, swaying at the end of a stretched neck and reminiscent of a Triffid or the plant Audrey II in *The Little Shop of Horrors*. Then is the time to feed this little monster with its first dollop of Glop. This may sound messy but you will soon discover that hand-feeding baby birds *is* messy. We feed all our orphans on good old St Tiggywinkles Glop, which we have always found to be a very successful diet, but there are other groups, especially those based in America, who favour their own recipes. Our criterion is that a baby bird, if being fed correctly, should produce a well-formed faecal sac and our Glop does appear to meet that requirement. I will go into the business of faecal sacs after we have first managed to get the food in the mouth end.

Once your orphan has presented his cavern of a mouth for feeding, take a narrow plastic coffee stirrer or blunted cocktail stick and, literally, ladle a blob of Glop right down the back of the throat. The bird should then automatically gulp and swallow it down. It often seems to be an immense struggle, with the bird's whole body in convulsions forcing the food down, but this is quite normal. (Some 'plastics' are almost transparent, so you can actually watch the food pass down the oesophagus on the right side of the neck, gradually filling its crop just above its shoulders.) The open mouth will be thrust at you again for the next helping and that is how it's going to be for the next two weeks – an ever-open cavern demanding feeding every time you pass the nest. But be careful, baby birds have no way of regulating their food intake and can be overfed. At each feeding session, stop offering food before the crop is full and bulging; little and often is the rule and although it's time-consuming it makes for healthier babies.

When feeding baby birds, always keep to hand a tub of 'baby wipes' and always clean the beak, face and eyes after each session. This helps prevent the build-up of bacteria in old food and stops the concretion of solidified Glop around the eyes and ears.

There is no need to give a baby bird anything to drink since there is sufficient moisture in the Glop, and a fatal risk that liquids will be inhaled and lead to pneumonia.

Until now I have labelled baby birds as perpetual feeding machines which take over your life. Quite honestly, although it is a commitment, it's really not that bad and as a bird grows there will be times when it can be left for longer periods between feeds. Although each orphan should be assessed as an individual, a good rule of thumb for a feeding regime could be as follows:

Feed from 6.00am until 10.00pm
Birds aged 1–4 days, every 10–15 minutes
Birds aged 5–9 days, every 15–20 minutes
Birds aged 10–14 days, every 30–45 minutes
Birds aged over 14 days, every 60 minutes as a supplement – they should be feeding themselves on either live food or seed as well.

Once a bird is feeding itself, the top-up supplement should be continued for at least a week.

As you start to feed your baby bird with your plastic coffee stirrer, always have to hand a plastic spoon for, after you have countered that initial demand of the gaping mouth and watched the food struggle down the transparent oesophagus, your orphan will suddenly thrust its bottom into the air and will squeeze out a capsule of faeces and urates which you will deftly catch in your plastic spoon.

Birds, when very young, have a wonderful system wherein their faeces are enclosed in a glutinous sac so that the parent bird puts the food in one end and removes the faecal sac from the other. Keeping the nest clean in this way helps keep the birds dry and retain their body heat; it will be necessary until the youngsters have some feathers and can perch when they will attempt to evacuate over the side of the nest, a messy business as the gelatinous sac ceases to form, meaning that you will have to pay closer attention to your cleaning regime.

The little faecal sac, while it appears, really is a marvel – not only does it keep the nest clean but it acts as a good barometer of the baby bird's condition. It should be well-formed and you should be able to pick the sac up with a pair of forceps or tweezers. Sometimes when an orphan first arrives, its faeces are liquid and messy, but after one or two days on a good diet, the sac should start to appear.

If, during the early stages of fostering, there is a failure to produce a faecal sac, this can be a sign that either there is something lacking in the diet or it may be an early warning of a gastro-intestinal upset. Put the baby back on to Lectade gavage for two to three hours, check the diet and then try again on solid food. If it does not improve then have a faecal sample checked for parasites or infection. Your vet should be able to do this and prescribe a suitable medication based on any findings. However, with a tiny bird, the balance between life and death is so minute that urgency is essential. In the meantime, you should maintain the bird's strength with alternate feeds of Lectade and Glop, or your own tried and tested recipe.

Weighing your bird at the same time every day will also give an indication of its well-being. For instance, a robin that will hatch at 1.7 gm will reach 18 gm in ten days and a starling hatching at 6 gm will reach 60 gm in the same period. Mind you, this is in the wild and we cannot possibly hope to emulate the growth rate of a parent-reared bird. All we can do is watch the weight and if an orphan maintains its weight and gradually adds the grammes, it stands a good chance of fledging successfully. If there is a weight loss, try increasing the number of feeds; not the amount given at each feed; check and, if necessary, turn up the heating or, once again, take a

A ruffled but perfectly healthy baby robin

faecal sample and check your diet formula.

In spite of all these precautions and even laboratory tests and medication, you will still get birds that die. This is going to happen, but as you become more experienced you will begin to notice the early-warning signs of problems – like the dry mucous membranes, or a tendency not to respond to feeding stimuli. Lectade will become the most crucial part of your first aid kit and gradually you will find that more and more orphans are surviving to the next stage of development: that of the nestling.

The one good thing with hatchlings is that they do not have their eyes open and do not have the horror of realising that their foster mother is a hulking great human. When they do open their eyes for the first time they im-

print on the first creature they see. That is to say, they take this as being the first sight of a parent. This happens with all species of wildlife and can be a problem if the orphan grows up assuming humans are adults of its species. I once heard of a kestrel chick being hatched and raised by a captive, much larger goshawk. Goshawks are the arch-killers of the birds of prey and used to be known as 'Cooks' hawks' because of all the game they caught for medieval tables. Because of the danger of this 'imprinted' kestrel approaching any other goshawk it had to be kept in captivity for its own safety.

As your hatchling imprints on you, it's your duty to handle the bird as little as possible, preferably to feed it through a screen, resisting the temptation to talk to it. In this way it will attain a certain amount of independence and, as it is a garden bird, it should not encounter problems like the kestrel. In fact, it has been proved that tame robins will nest and breed quite naturally. However, never strive to tame a bird before release, but by all means make a friend of it once it is wild and free.

Looking after a nestling

The nestling, when it arrives, will have its eyes already open and will be imprinted on its natural parents. One look at you will send it into instant panic, resulting in an extremely unco-operative, stubborn bundle of miserable feathers, with its beak clamped firmly shut.

Fledglings, once settled, can be encouraged to feed

You can try tapping its beak to encourage it to gape and accept food and even try putting it with other birds which readily accept food. Normally, gentle persuasion does not work but I have found that if you force-feed the first one or two mouthfuls, the orphan seems to realise suddenly that you are a ready meal and is soon gaping every time it sees you.

Force-feeding brings images of suffragettes

LEFT *Healthy appetites are a sure sign that the babies are on the mend*

and stomach tubes, but it's nowhere near as drastic. Take the bird in your left hand with the index finger lying along the edge of the beak. With the thumb nail of your right hand gently prise the beak open (the bottom beak is the only part that moves) and hold it open with the waiting index finger of the left hand. Now spatula your blob of Glop into the back of the throat, let the beak go and let the bird swallow. Put it back in the cage and try tapping the beak, on the phalanges, with your spatula of Glop. On most occasions it will gape, but if not, force-feed again in ten minutes.

With nestlings you will not get the pre-packed faecal sac, so be prepared to change the paper towels at each feeding.

Looking after a fledgling

In the final stage of a young bird's development it becomes a fledgling, when it will have a complete complement of feathers, although they will not be as fully developed as those of an adult bird. This is the phase when many young birds leave the nest to secrete themselves around the garden. These fledglings are the bundles of feathers with no tails but apparently extremely long legs that are regularly being picked up as helpless orphans, when in fact they are doing very well.

As they come into care they will often panic at your first attempts to feed them. Try the one-off force-feeding technique and see if they will gape. If they do agree to feed, then many of them will be on the point of weaning and will clumsily attempt to peck the Glop off the spatula, spattering it over themselves, their cage and you. It's a very frustrating exercise trying to feed these 'teenagers', but try taking advantage of their efforts and give them a dish of Glop on which to practise their pecking. This is also the time to offer a small bowl of live food: either mini-mealworms or white, cleaned 'pinkies', which are small maggots available at angling shops. The movement of the live food may just entice them to start

pecking and, provided that multi-vitamins are added to the bowl then you are on the last lap leading up to release of your baby birds.

Smaller birds like tits, wrens and fly-catchers can be offered twigs covered with aphids, one of the reasons why I grow elder-berry and nasturtiums for their inevitable infestations. The flycatchers will also start performing their dainty aerobatics by hawking any fly that happens to pass through their cage.

Gradually remove any heating from the cages then, after a couple of days, it is necessary to put your charges into larger, outside flight cages so that they can exercise their muscles to flying efficiency. However, keep an eye on the weather just in case a cold shower gets through to one of the young birds, causing hypothermia.

Releasing young birds

Finally, early on a dry warm day, let your birds free into your garden, offering them bowls of food outside their flight cage. Some will simply fly off to join their wild cousins, while others, such as the blackbirds and robins, may well avail themselves of your hospitality until the following spring sees them off trying to find a mate.

Any migratory birds – swallows, martins, flycatchers and cuckoos – should never be released after September, as any adverse weather conditions on the flight south may be just more than they can cope with. Keep these

Food Chart for Baby Birds

**Defrosted Frozen Mice
or Day-old Chicks**

Hawks
Owls
Falcons
Gulls
Corvids

**Chick Crumbs
and Fresh Water**

Ducks
Geese
Swans

**Sprats and
Thiamine Supplement**

Seabirds
Herons

**Complan and
Dry Porridge Oats**

Pigeons
Doves

**Whitebait and
Thiamine Supplement**

Grebes
Kingfishers
Small Fish-eaters

WHT Glop

Passerines
(Garden birds)
Corvids
(crows etc.)
Hirundines
(Swallows, martins etc.)

**Small, Clean White
Maggots, Pinkies
or Mealworms**

Moorhens
Coots
Insectivores

---

over the winter then release them when the migrants return the following spring.

I am writing this in September when our major influx of baby birds is over, although there are still a few pigeons coming in. I have a young cuckoo which I am having to over-winter on its own, but the winter migrant fieldfare I have had all summer can now look forward to the imminent arrival of its cousins from Scandinavia.

We are still rearing baby squirrels, glis glis and hedgehogs, who will soon be old enough to feed themselves so that, during the winter, we can concentrate on cold weather casualties and urge everybody to keep their bird tables topped up with good garden-bird fare.

Postscript

Once your bird garden is functioning and flourishing, you will be amazed at the amount of animal traffic that passes through. The pond at first light will be a metropolis of starlings bathing, dragonflies shimmering their wings to catch the sun's first warmth and swallows and martins swooping down to catch the first midges. A cock blackbird will be sitting on the highest branch singing his heart out and he has probably been there since before dawn. His mate sitting with only the top of her head showing, on her nest in the climber by the patio, is obviously a little annoyed at 'jenny wren' fussing about above her head looking for spiders. A chipping sound by the path attracts your attention to a song thrush smashing a snail to pieces on the hard stone while a little dunnock surreptitiously creeps up behind to steal morsels of the unfortunate mollusc as they fly in all directions.

This scenario continues from dawn till dusk. A continually changing hive of activity and interest that demands your constant attention. So, if like me, you work at a desk and have to concentrate, I would strongly advise against sitting facing a window on to this wonderful scene. Mind you, it does no harm to take the occasional sneaking look, even if it does keep you spellbound for the next few hours.

The Wildlife Hospital Trust (St Tiggywinkles) has now taken the step of building Europe's first Wildlife Teaching Hospital so we may pass on to others what we have learned. We run day courses in the care of sick, injured or orphaned wild birds. We are a registered charity and if you would like more information on the Trust's educational programme, would like to make a donation, or more importantly, want help with injured wild birds, please write, with a stamped addressed envelope, or phone to:

The Wildlife Hospital Trust (St Tiggywinkles)
Department C.G.B.
Aylesbury, Bucks HP21 7NY
Telephone 0296 29860

We also publish information on drugs and dosages for British wildlife. Please ask for our publications list.

Bibliography

Armstrong, E. A., *The Folklore of Birds*, Collins, 1958

Baines, C., *How to Make a Wildlife Garden*, Elm Tree Books, 1985

Bickerton, W., *The Baby Bird and its Problems*, Methuen, 1927

Bolund, L., *Nest Boxes for the Birds of Britain and Europe*, Sainsbury, 1987

Coles, B. H., *Avian Medicine and Surgery*, Blackwell Scientific, 1985

Cooper, John, *First Aid and Care of Wild Birds*, David and Charles, 1983

Dougall, R., *A Celebration of Birds*, Collins, 1978

Douglas-Home, H., *The Birdman*, Collins, 1977

Feare, C. J., *The Starling*, Shire Natural History, 1985

Flegg, J., *A Notebook of Birds 1907–1980*, Macmillan, 1981

Genders, R., *Wildlife in the Garden*, Faber & Faber, 1976

Gibbons, B. L., *Creating a Wildlife Garden*, Hamlyn, 1988

Glue, D., *The Garden Bird Book*, Macmillan, 1988

Goodwin, D., *Birds of Man's World*, British Museum Publications, 1978

Greenoak, F., *All the Birds of the Air*, André Deutsch, 1979

Grey of Fallodon, *The Charm of Birds*, Hodder & Stoughton, 1927

Harrison, C., *A Field Guide to the Nests, Eggs and Nestlings of British and European Birds*, Collins, 1975

Hole, C., *English Folklore*, Batsford, 1940

Howard, L., *Birds as Individuals*, Collins, 1952

Howes, F. N., *Plants and Beekeeping*, Faber & Faber, 1945

King, A. S. & McLelland, J., *Birds, Their Structure and Function*, Baillière, Tindall, 1984.

Knight, M., *Bird Gardening*, Routledge & Kegan Paul, 1954

Lack, D., *The Life of the Robin*, Witherby, 1965

Mead, C., *Robins*, Whittet, 1984

Mockler, M., *Birds in the Garden*, Blandford, 1982

Murray, W. J. C., *A Sanctuary Planted*, Country Book Club, 1954

Oddie, W. E., *Bill Oddie's Little Black Bird Book*, Methuen, 1980

Parkin, R. & A., *Countryside Garden*, Johnsons Seeds

Rothschild, M. & Clay, T., *Fleas, Flukes and Cuckoos*, Collins, 1953

Snow, D. W., *The Blackbird*, Shire Natural History, 1987

Soper, T., *Wildlife Begins at Home*, David & Charles, 1975

Soper, T., *Discovering Birds*, BBC Publications, 1983

Staples, C. Percival, *Birds in a Garden Sanctuary*, Warne, 1946

Tate, P., *The Swallow*, Shire Natural History, 1986

Temple, J., *Worm Compost*, Soil Association, 1979

Tudor, A. M., *A Little Book of Birds and Beasts*, Medici Society

Turner, E. L., *Every Garden a Bird Sanctuary*, Witherby, 1935

Universities Federation of Animal Welfare, *The Ecology and Control of Feral Cats*, 1980

Wood, N., *Birds in Your Garden*, Hamlyn, 1985

Index